CONCILIUM

THEOLOGY IN THE AGE OF RENEWAL

CONCILIUM

CONCILIUM/VOL. 42

LITURGY

THE CRISIS OF LITURGICAL REFORM

VOLUME 42

CONCILIUM
theology in the age of renewal

PAULIST PRESS

NEW YORK, N.Y. / GLEN ROCK, N.J.

PAULIST PRESS
EXECUTIVE OFFICES: 304 W. 58th Street, New York, N.Y. and 21
   Harristown Road, Glen Rock, N.J.
Publisher: John A. Carr, C.S.P.

EDITORIAL OFFICES: 304 W. 58th Street, New York, N.Y.
Executive Editor: Kevin A. Lynch, C.S.P.
Managing Editor: Urban P. Intondi

Printed and bound in the United States of America by
Wickersham Printing Co., Lancaster, Pa.

CONTENTS

PREFACE

To many outsiders the partial liturgical reforms brought in after Vatican Council II look somewhat insignificant and uncoordinated. This staggered procedure hardly provides a clear idea of what the liturgy must be in the future. The Council's intention was definitely not to make isolated changes but rather to bring about an "aggiornamento" of that complex whole which we call "liturgy". There is therefore every justification for an investigation of what should be the guiding principle for this aggiornamento. Moreover, this principle itself cannot be something static; it has to take account of the actual situation in which the modern practicing Catholic finds himself. This situation does not permit a long, drawn-out dawdling. On the other hand, however, the situation can never be so alarming that we have to plunge into arbitrary improvization in such an important matter. This paradoxical situation can be described by Chesterton's words: "When Rome burns, it is high time to study the laws of hydraulic power."

This dilemma about the future of the liturgy is the basic theme of this volume. Even the liturgy itself is no longer something obvious. The future of the liturgy can no longer be simply deduced from the assertion that man is by nature "liturgical". Basic reflection on the nature, necessity and structure of the liturgy is

1

essential if we want to undertake this all-embracing task of its reform with any hope of success.

In order to avoid the quicksands of pure theory, it was deemed necessary not to limit ourselves to this basic reflection but also to have a close look at those liturgical reforms that have already been achieved in the short period after Vatican Council II. This study indicates that the need for a reform is not peculiar to Catholicism. Other Christian Churches, such as the Anglican and the Calvinist communities, appear to be just as preoccupied with a fundamental revision of their liturgy. At the fourth Assembly of the World Council of Churches last year at Uppsala, this item appeared on the agenda for the first time. It is no longer possible to conceal the fact that several Churches seem to be rather tired of this liturgy problem. On the other hand, the religious possibilities of more contemporary forms of expression such as jazz and folk rock have been recognized, and their use justifies the hope that the creative potential of the modern Christian is vital enough to overcome the crisis in our present liturgical life.

In the first article Vilanova links this liturgical crisis with the fact that religion has lost that aspect of being taken for granted which supported it for centuries. Then McNamara tries to discover some solution in the liturgical practice of the first Christians. A close look shows that the present tendency to desacralize the liturgy does not differ as much as we might think from the tendencies that animated the liturgies of the first ten centuries. In both cases it is the ordinary "concrete" things in man's existence which are taken to symbolize and express the element of holiness. In the cosmocentric view of man of earlier days, the accent fell on the tangible elements in the great world of creation —water, ointment, incense and icons—and all that was materially observable was seized upon in order to express the Invisible. In the anthropocentric view of the man of today, the emphasis falls on ethical values—justice and love—and so today it is those values in creation that are experienced as manifesting the Invisible.

Meyer tries to find the norm which presided over the changes in the liturgy that have already been put into practice. Marsili shows that the problem of the vernacular in the liturgy is not solved merely by translating the texts of the Roman liturgy. Language is something more than the mere means of interpreting ideas: it presupposes a whole culture and a view of man that were prevalent in a given age. The Documentation section delves still further into this thorny problem of religious language.

Since liturgy leans heavily on man's creativity and his artistic gifts (how many works of art in music, painting and sculpture have not been produced by twenty centuries of Christianity!) it is obvious that the problem of the future of the liturgy implies an examination of the function of music in its classical and modern forms (Stefani and Hucke). McDonnell, Lescrauwaet and Buchanan point to what is useful for a Catholic liturgical reform in the Calvinist approach to a liturgy which shows the same elements of crisis, and in the attempts made in this field by the Anglicans and the World Council of Churches.

After this general reconnaissance of the problem, Rennings presents some cautious indications for the future. Originally this volume was meant to include a contribution about the relationship between the secular and the sacred, but since the volume dealing with Church history will tackle this issue extensively from its historical background, this present liturgical volume only refers to it *en passant,* and we refer the reader to Volume 47 which will appear later this year. We hope, however, that what is offered here will show that there is a way out of the present impasse of our liturgy. The fact that the way to the future of the liturgy is not yet wholly clear seemed to us no reason why we should not trace its beginnings.

PART I
ARTICLES

Evangelista Vilanova, O.S.B./*Barcelona, Spain*

The Liturgical Crisis and Criticism of Religion

The post-conciliar liturgical reform, with the introduction of living languages and some discreet simplifications and modifications of rites, has brought an unexpected phenomenon to light. The fact that the people now understand the liturgy better has shown that the adaptations made since the Council have not been as radical as many of the faithful needed; the categories are still the same, even though the forms may be different. Traditional liturgy uses an inherited language which man today finds anachronistic and artificial, to the extent that it is often judged to belong to the mythology of previous generations. (It is possible, for example, that failure to distinguish between biblical and poetical-liturgical language can lead people to discover that the liturgical assembly is a regression from the exegetical conclusions found in biblical study groups to archaic and even mythological conceptions of the texts it uses.) Men today therefore find liturgical language and the ideas it contains, and even the very symbolism of the liturgy, empty of content and largely meaningless to those who live in an industrial and urban civilization.

But the fact that there is a liturgical crisis cannot be attributed to the language factor alone. There are many other causes, dormant for some time, which are now becoming intensely obvious. There is, for example, the reaction against conformity to a ritual whose content no longer responds to the spiritual needs of the time. If the effort at renewal, still in its infancy, has not yet managed to give the real meaning of the liturgy back to many people—the faithful included—it has at least shown that the real liturgical crisis must be seen as part of a "more extensive crisis".[1]

This crisis concerns the "God-man" relationship in the first place, and the "Church-world" relationship in the second. In the final analysis it is really the image of God that is in question. If the "process of secularization" we are going through means that the constituent realities of human life can be established without reference to God, it is readily understandable that the term "liturgy" is unlikely to arouse much interest in modern man, secularized as he is to a greater or lesser degree. If he has freed himself from the "God-hypothesis", he will also have freed himself from the fear that formerly found expression in rites of expiation, propitiation and petition. The advances of civilization and technology have procured certain basic securities that formerly had to be sought through the liturgy.

To move from the present situation to the thought that produced it can be very instructive here. Christianity, along with all other religions, has been the object of an intellectual assault with few precedents. Historical and psychological criticism has tried to reduce religion to a mechanism of illusion or evasion. For the great adversaries of religion, Nietzsche, Marx and Freud, religion is fear, using God or any other superhuman force to make up for the ignorance or impotence of humanity in its infancy or adolescence. Now that mankind has come of age, it can free itself from the liturgical or moral aids of religion that were useful while it lacked power itself. There is no explanation for the survival of religion in the age of mankind's scientific maturity. This is why today man no longer feels "religious".

But it is precisely this fact, which worries so many Christians, that gives us the occasion to show greater fidelity to the Gospel. Because the much criticized concept of "religion" has been out-

---

[1] P. Vanbergen, "La crise de la liturgie: aspects d'une crise plus vaste," in *Paroisse et Liturgie* 49 (1967), pp. 642-59.

grown, a common denominator going beyond confessional con-
flicts is making its presence felt in Christian theology. Let us not
forget the prophetic denunciations of religion made by the great
Christian theologian Karl Barth, and by Deitrich Bonhoeffer.
With them, criticism of religion springs from the Gospel, from
the very bowels of Christianity itself.

Barth characterizes ambiguity as an essential mark of religion.
Any religious element—including the liturgy—has, on the one
hand, its basis and invisible meaning in God, and so finds its
value in him. But it is at the same time an historical and psychological reality—in other words, a human possibility, and thus
one belonging to the world of sin. One proceeds on the right
track by recognizing this basic ambiguity of religion and liturgy.
Christ came to judge religion, which means to condemn it, and
also to save it. This salvation comes about through faith.

I
"FAITH-RELIGION": A FRUITFUL DISTINCTION

To try simply to oppose faith and religion, as some have done,
perhaps for the ecumenical reason of reproducing the spirit of
the Reformed tradition, runs the risk of falling into superficiality.
History and anthropology both show the impossibility of transmitting faith in its pure and abstract state. It always takes place
in the context—a humiliating context if you like—of a definite
"religion". Neither faith nor religion has ever existed pure and
simple. The difference between primitive Christianity and Con-
stantinism is only the inversion of the dominant aspect.

The Sunday celebration is a good example of this. In the last
years before the Edict of Constantine, Christian literature shows
a certain coolness toward the festive idea of Sunday; the spirit of
"religion" and of "carrying out religious duties" was already
clouding the joyful vision of the old Sunday. After the Edict, the
aspect of a "day of worship" of the divinity, a day set aside for
"religious obligations", was felt in all its force. The eucharist,
which until then had been experienced as a sign of the victory of

the Lord, came to be considered as primarily the sacrificial offering which replaced the old pagan sacrifices. One could even say that the revelation of the Good News was interpreted on the plane of natural religiosity.

From that time on, the Church has been more and more closely involved in institutionalized religion, with the best and the worst that the phenomenon of institutionalization brings with it. Among the worst we must certainly include the tendency to convert means into an end, and the liturgy, the ritual means of communing with God, has not escaped the danger. Whenever liturgy gives external practices a value beyond what they possess, it must be criticized and purged of all practices that can appear idolatrous, superstitious and formalistic. This critical function belongs to faith, which ultimately must motivate liturgical expressions.

In this context, faith and religion will not end by producing competing rival interpretations, one of which could eliminate the other. There must be dialectical relationships of mutual criticism woven between them, and each must prevent the other from becoming hardened into a system. It is not a question of devaluing ritual in the name of faith or the Word, as was done in primitive Protestantism, but of developing the potential of rituals by means of faith, so that they cease to be simply elements of a religious cult and become effective signs of the mystery of Christ.

It is true that there is a form of worship stemming from man's natural inclinations, from his fear of God, which invokes God as an answer to man's problems. This worship is guilty of a series of degradations of the evangelical understanding of God, easily degenerating into magic or superstition.

This fact is the result of the ambiguity of religion and is not sufficient reason for us to reject every kind of worship. There is also the worship that stems from faith, which in the terminology of the New Testament we call liturgy, based on the hearing of the Word of God revealed in Christ. To get an adequate answer to our problem we must consider Christian liturgy as the expression of man's religious nature and *at the same time* as the historical manifestation of the mystery of Christ.

Nature and history must be the two sources of all celebrations: by complementing each other they will avoid the possible rift between ritual and its content of living faith, and achieve an admittedly difficult harmony. Let us remember that if at times liturgical expressions have been detrimental to the life of faith, it is quite possible that today the life of faith is devaluing liturgical expression. This is where we should find the meaning of Bonhoeffer's expression "religionless Christianity", which he himself did not explain adequately. If it means purging Christianity of all man's efforts to justify himself to himself, then it can be fruitful. But if it means eliminating the possibility of man responding to grace through the signs of the Church, then it would be overthrowing Christian revelation itself.

II
A LITURGY OVERBURDENED WITH "RELIGIOUS" CONCEPTS?

Accepting, with the necessary qualifications, that there is a contrast between "faith" and "religion", we can now pick out some "religious" concepts that, among others, should be criticized in the way the prophets attacked idols or the first Christian preachers spoke out against pagan superstitions. This must be done if we are to prevent the Christian liturgy from degenerating into a caricature of itself.

Justification through Ritual

History proves that there has been a constant temptation for Christianity to be reduced to a process of fulfilling external observances (moral commands) and carrying out rituals, to the detriment of an evangelical approach. In liturgy, the danger is toward the production of a series of rigid, lifeless scenes. In practice, concession to this ritualism creates the "practicing" type, who is not always the same as the "believing" type. The practicing type usually feels the need for "security" in relation to the beyond, because he believes that the sacramental life can give him this security. His religious piety, often based on a severe conception of God, exists in the context of an archaic sort of fear. This leads him to turn to rites in search of his individual "eternal salvation" and sometimes also in search of his "personal fulfillment" in this world. Without being aware of it, he is then guilty of the sin of "magic", which consists in using God as a dispensation from resolving his personal problems himself. And in fact liturgy will be magic if it is practiced as a substitute for the free and personal efforts owed by everyone to the creation of a more just world.

One cannot insist too strongly on the fact that it is not the simple practice of ritual that justifies man, but the gratuitous intervention of God which makes it possible for the actions of a believer, within a community of faith that lives the sacramental mystery of Christ, to lead to salvation. Perhaps what we need to avoid ritualistic dangers is a precise historical explanation, free from any polemical overtone, of the meaning of *opus operatum*.

The Danger of Alienation

A liturgy whose exclusive preoccupation seems to be with its own development, away from man's creative involvement in other areas of life, cannot call itself especially "Christian". We need a basic revision of our liturgy if it is not to alienate men by cutting them off from the world. The specific forms with which most of us have to live have taken on an alienating character which has contributed to the separation of liturgical life from everyday life. This is the natural consequence of the "religious" mentality, which sets a gulf between the sacred and the profane. Religion, by setting aside special places, particular times, ornaments and so on as its special preserve, creates a world apart which for most people is not a real expression of human life. To try to contain religion exclusively within the confines of this sacred, set-apart world prevents the profane spheres of life from maintaining any relationship with God. In the "sacred space" of a church, for example, people are conscious that they are experiencing something "religious" outside their own world and experience of life; they do not know how to connect the words and rites of "church" to their real needs and hopes. Sunday, taken by religion as "sacred time", helps to create an abyss between what we might call the day of the Lord, with its obligation to worship, and the day of man, with its aspirations to freedom and leisure.

The result of all this is that many, not excluding priests themselves, use their dedication to the liturgy to justify remaining aloof from the real concerns of their brothers. Offering up petitions allows them to attribute their failure to achieve something through their own efforts to the will of God, instead of sharing the sensitivity of Christ, who is present in the humble and needy. It is characteristic of some "religious professionals" to behave as if they had never heard the imprecations launched by Amos and Isaiah against useless sacrifices as a remedy for lapses in justice or love.

Eschatological Anticipation

Religion (the Church herself, according to Bonhoeffer), runs the risk of being satisfied with the contemplation of its own existence, and forgetting that it must have its sights set on God and serve its Lord. Liturgy can never be its own ultimate end: its truth is in man, for whom it is celebrated, in the world, which through Christ is going toward God. The first Christians realized the provisional character of the liturgy, and medieval theology formulated it, in its own terms, by explaining that it belongs to the "order of signs".

But history shows that eucharistic worship, for example, has often tended to treat the eucharist as an end, when it is only the means to our union with the Father. When this happens, sacramental progress in relation to the final realities comes to a halt; liturgy loses its historic and dynamic force and becomes a "thing", static and complete in itself. This tendency is strengthened by the hostility to evolution produced by ritualist dogmatism, and the fact is that this approach is irrelevant to the needs of the faithful who live in a dialectic of crises—crises of adolescence, crises brought about by particular circumstances, even crises brought about by doubtful propositions. Under the umbrella of rite, people run the risk of standing still. A baptized person is a baptized person, a communion is a communion, a marriage is a marriage. If one is too anxious to make sure that he possesses the appropriate rites, he only sees them as fixed and immovable once and forever. He fails to see the spiritual progressions or human regressions behind the rites, or attached to them, or the contributions, often rich in vitality, other times poor, of the faith that shows or seems to show itself under the uniform covering of these same rites.

It would be a mistake to forget that the liturgy, while it is based on the invisible presence of God, has to feel his absence also. A tension between presence and absence of God saves the liturgy from all attempts by the forces of "religion" to turn it into an eschatological end in itself.

All-Pervading Legalism

The Bible invites us to praise God for his marvels. This invitation is expressed chiefly in worship. Praise is the highest expression of worship. Thus the eucharist is presented as a "sacrifice of praise" in which the faithful, in the words of the introductory dialogue to the Preface, are invited to take part.

To pass from this invitation to the obligation of attending Mass every Sunday is the work of a "religious" legalism unknown to the primitive Church. Invitation has been changed into precept. It could be argued that a precept is more effective than an invitation, but it is possible that obligation, a juridical and moral qualification, may have prejudiced the understanding of the Mass to the extent that its essential meaning has been deformed. It has led to the predominance of aspects other than praise and the action of grace: the need for expiation and propitiation, characteristics of sacrifice, and prayers of petition.

The Sunday obligation has marked the consciences of many of the faithful in a particular way, by producing a fear complex toward the sin they would commit by failing to attend Mass; in the same way it quiets the consciences of many "practicing Catholics" who carry out their Sunday duties from the thoroughly ungenerous motive of avoiding sin. Obsession with the obligation results in the Mass becoming an exercise of virtue and obedience, perhaps even a penitential exercise. Thus it loses the spontaneity essential to a real personal encounter with God in Christ, and to the lyricism of praise of the *mirabilia Dei*.

III
LITURGY AS A REQUIREMENT OF FAITH

Preoccupation with "sacramentalizing" has led many priests to summon everyone to liturgical observance without stopping to think of the approaches and development necessary for participation in the liturgical assembly. This needs a life of faith in a continual process of education and development on both individual and community levels. Faith alone can overcome the "religious" dangers that we have pointed out. This is because faith begins by teaching us that the Word of God is not an "answer" to the questions posed by the human condition. Liturgy, based on this Word, includes rather a question put to man by God, a question which prevents us from living in the cocoon of safety in which we are enclosed by rites and a domesticated faith.

God's Gift Is Gratuitous

The "believer", instructed by the Word of God, will realize that the way he thinks about God will depend on the focus of the liturgy itself. A more evangelical idea of God requires a more spiritual and disinterested form of worship. Where the Christian liturgy is concerned, this means that it will not consist in "proferring honors to the deity, but in receiving, in faith and the action of grace, the saving acts of God in Jesus Christ". God takes the initiative in saving, a process which, as the medieval theologians tell us, is not necessarily linked to sacramental rites. God keeps his freedom; he permits himself to be met by those who seek him with faith, but he does not allow himself to be used as a magic intervener, making up for human laziness by dispensing men from their duty of achievement.

The role of the priest as prophet and teacher fits him for proclaiming that God's gratuitous saving action is not in competiton with man's achievements. Thus, at a pace suited to his community, he should enable his people to progressively discover the true significance of the various gestures and signs of the liturgy. In this way the community will progress from a magic ritual to one which, without assuring anything, expresses a lively faith in a God, who is *semper maior,* who cannot be reduced to an institutional level, a God who has to be new every day. This will prevent such attitudes as those of many Spanish peasants who attribute good harvests to the fact that the land has been blessed. To have recourse to sacramental rites to further worldly interests is not the attitude of faith, but an insult to the gratuitousness of God.

The De-Alienating Function of Faith

If the liturgy can be criticized as alienating, this is due to the fact that it has been insufficiently enlivened by faith. A liturgy which thinks of itself as being primarily a "service to the sacred", to "religious" values, will always be a partial act, incapable of relating to the totality of human life. This is why we are now lamenting the divorce of the liturgy from daily life.

The same could not be said of a liturgy that was a true expression of faith. Faith is a total act. It is the starting point for recapturing the real meaning of liturgy in secular life itself. Man will then be a true *liturgos* to the extent that he takes on the tasks that define him as a man. Spiritual sacrifice, of which tradition speaks, and which takes in the whole of human existence, is an integrating part of the liturgy and its true fruit.

Liturgical self-satisfaction must give way to projection of the liturgy toward others, toward the real world. In the life of the "believer", everything starts from the altar and everything leads to the altar. The presentation of the mystery of Christ in the eucharist is at the beginning and the end of his actions. This eucharist is not a meeting with God on the fringe of the world, as it were, but the taking up of the interests of this world suffering and working for its fulfillment. The step from ritualism to service should be the ripe fruit of faith expressed in the sacrament.

When this happens it will be much easier for the celebrations, under a legitimate diversity of forms, to show forth the deeply genuine "worldly" attitude (in the sense of feeling concern for the world) of the Christian liturgy. This is why faith has a right to criticize liturgy, since it inevitably tends to incorporate elements of natural religion and so tends to reduce our relationship to God to a series of demands expressed in ritual form. Faith shows us that God wants more from man than these demands: he wants us to take up our total calling as human beings, in a spirit of solidarity with our brothers.

The Historical Value of the Liturgy

It is now generally held that the individual is integrated into the history of salvation through faith and the sacraments of faith, baptism and the eucharist in particular. This history is not a past reality, but the present place in which we communicate with God. Thus it is pastorally very important to emphasize the historical value of faith and the sacraments.

Faith is not a choice made once and forever. We do not suddenly decide one day to be "believers". It is a choice we have to make every day in the face of God who takes us by surprise.

The liturgy, particularly the eucharist, commemorates a past event, the death and resurrection of the Lord, *donec veniat*. The Church, imprisoned in the exodus of human history, has the task of connecting men of today, of every age, with the central mystery of saving history. Liturgical celebration can have no other end: this is why it is the *fons et culmen* of the activity of the Church, "the sacrament of universal salvation".

This historical character explains why the liturgy should always leave us with a feeling of dissatisfaction: its end being transcendent, it can never be reached in its full and fulfilling form. It gives us the presence of God *in mysterio,* but also makes us feel his absence, a sign of the visible absence of God in the world, a certain "uselessness" of God in history. The feeling of deprivation this imposes makes the believer one with all men who are searching, and more understanding toward the atheist who lives, as it were, deprived of God.

This attitude, the opposite of pharisaical self-satisfaction, will help us to feel that "before God and with God, we live without God", as Bonhoeffer put it. This outlook can be the source of a dynamism that the modern world cannot overlook. This is where the value of the prophetic function can be seen: thanks to the Word, it interiorizes and personalizes the liturgy, forming it into evangelical attitudes and pushing it into vital choices in the network of its everyday relationships; it can awaken spiritual anxieties, questions and replies to the interrogations of the Lord in our lives.

Liturgy as the Sacrament of Faith

To hear the Word of the saving God brings relief from the old dreads that assailed primitive humanity. The biblical account of the *mirabilia Dei,* continued in the liturgy and in the signs of the times, "signs of the presence of God", makes the believer feel a spontaneous need to praise and to thank. It is a matter of supreme moment for him to unite himself to Christ's praising and giving thanks, commemorated in the eucharist. Without needing rules, which belong more properly to an infantile stage of humanity and not to the law of Christ, a law of grace, love and filial freedom, he feels the imperative of his own faith (what Barth calls the "prophetic imperative") impelling him to unite himself with a particular Mass-celebrating community.

If the faithful came to Mass not to avoid sin or to "practice" their religion, but under an impulse of freedom, love and compelling passion, the celebration would gain in truth, in intensity and in unity. Many people nowadays would like to see the obligation "under pain of grave sin"—more favorable to the development of a Church rich in numbers than of one rich in faith —gradually replaced by an education in faith that would form Christians in a consciousness of their freedom as sons of God. Today the need for catechesis is so great that, in view of the amount of time people have available, it perhaps argues for a reduction in the number of liturgical services. Needless to say, this would prepare the way for simplification of proceedings and rites, and, in the extreme case where a minimum of lived faith was lacking, require refusal to administer the sacraments. Is this not the real conclusion to which we are forced by the traditional concept of the Church as the sacrament of faith?

IV

CONCLUSIONS

Faith in this context has the difficult but possible task of disentangling the common confusions between what is essential in the liturgy and a Mass of "religious", excessively human, illusions. Faith "comes from what is heard" (Rom. 10. 19), and so perhaps the first conclusion we should come to is an insistence on the prophetic role of the Word in liturgical celebrations. In the "sacrament-Word" binomial there is the balance between permanence and change, between institution and happening. This means that the Word must not become just another rite, intelligible only to the initiated, but a prophetic force like that in the Old Testament, proclaiming a "religion in life and in history", a religion very attentive to the social relationships of justice and brotherhood, seen in the light of the demands of God's covenant and justice. Unless it adopts these attitudes, our liturgy will be a false one.

The prophetic Word demands the response of faith not only in the action of the liturgy, but also in the course of the events that make up the history of everyday life. In this way the liturgy, which enshrines so many traditional values, will also listen to the new demands, tackle the problems of the moment and feel itself open to new forms. When this happens, perhaps we shall be able to talk of a collective prophetic office which—without excluding the role to be played by particular outstanding personalities—will be able to make the force of its communal faith felt and thus, its faith matured by habitual participation, take the initiative in introducing reforms.

But before we reach this stage—and this is my second conclusion—the priest will have to become a true teacher. We need instruction in faith, which has to come before celebration. One can guess at what this instruction in integration—which, without denigrating the decidedly ambiguous virtues of popular faith, will purify them and make the liturgy their logical outcome—will involve.

Could this program which I have barely sketched resolve the present liturgical crisis? The pointers I have given could be taken as leading to a vicious circle. The advancement of faith will give back to our liturgy the purity and simplicity that will make it acceptable to our contemporaries. But the liturgical crisis is often also the "crisis of faith", a far wider crisis which does not always spring from the same reasons as the liturgical crisis, but often co-exists with it and sometimes, at crucial moments, interferes with it, because it shares the same anthropological problematic, which has to do with transcendence.

Once the crisis of personal faith can be resolved, the way is mapped out. The liturgy, purified by a criticism of religion which will bring about the advancement of faith, will be renewed for the Christian community in its inner life, and will then be capable of putting modern man in contact with the Church and, through the Church, with God. In the new "secularized" world, God will better be able to be God than he has been, precisely to the degree that religion gives way to faith. Faith will ensure that what emerges from criticism of religion, and from the liturgical crisis in particular, will not necessarily be negative. The religious consciousness of humanity probably needs to pass through this moment of darkness in order to better appreciate the image of God presented in the gospels, an image obscured by a worship dominated by natural aspects of our relations with the divinity. The result of this process will help to form a Church of true worshipers of the Father in spirit and in truth (Jn. 4, 23).

Martin McNamara, M.S.C./*Ballyglunin, Ireland*

The Liturgical Assemblies
and Religious Worship of
the Early Christians[1]

"No student of liturgiology will need to be reminded that each of the great centers of Christianity evolved its own type of liturgy. But attempts to trace these back to their earliest form suggest that, apart from a very few constant features, there existed a maximum of freedom and diversity in the earliest period." So wrote Canon B. H. Streeter in 1929.[2] This article is devoted to a consideration of the worship of Christians during the earliest period of all—i.e. during the apostolic age.

There are a number of reasons why one should pay special attention to the liturgical assemblies of this period and to this earliest Christian worship. To begin with, in worship—as in other matters—the Church looks to the apostolic community as her model[3] and keeps it before her mind in liturgical renewal. Then again, this period of origins has its place in the history of the liturgy. Finally, the worshiping community played an impor-

[1] For further information on this subject, cf. H. Chirat, *L'assemblée chrétienne à l'âge apostolique* (Paris, 1949); O. Cullmann, *Early Christian Worship* (London, 1953); G. Delling, *Worship in the New Testament* (London, 1962); C. F. D. Moule, *Worship in the N.T.* (London, 1961); M. Goguel, *L'Église Primitive* (Paris, 1947), pp. 266-440. Current literature can be found in the *Elenchus Bibliographicus* XV, 16 of *Biblica*.

[2] *The Primitive Church* (London, 1929), p. 52.

[3] Cf. *Constitution on the Sacred Liturgy*, n. 6.

tant part in the formation of the New Testament, a good part of which was lived in the Christian assemblies before being consigned to writing.

I
WORSHIP IN SPIRIT AND IN TRUTH

It is scarcely necessary to remind the reader that what information the New Testament writings give on the liturgical assemblies and religious worship of the early Church is incidental —one could almost say accidental. We have, of course, in the New Testament ample material for a theology of Christian worship. God wills that those who worship him do so in spirit and in truth. Together with the ministering priesthood of Aaron, the Jews knew of another priesthood of all Israel, a priesthood conferred on the nation at the Sinai Covenant.[4] This privilege, too, the New Israel of God possesses. Christians are a royal priesthood,[5] a holy priesthood to offer spiritual sacrifices acceptable to God through Jesus Christ.[6]

On this spiritual worship the New Testament has much to say either explicitly or implicitly; on liturgical assemblies and the actual forms of worship it says but little. We get but fleeting glimpses of the early Church at worship. This lack of information invites speculation, a procedure not always indulged in with the happiest of results. In the present article it is intended to remain as factual as possible, giving what the New Testament record has to say and referring the reader to other sources for more detailed information on the subjects treated.

[4] Ex. 19, 6; 2 Mac. 2, 17; cf. M. McNamara, *The New Testament and the Palestinian Targum to the Pentateuch* (Rome, 1966), pp. 227-30.
[5] 1 Pet. 2, 1.
[6] 1 Pet. 2, 5; cf. Rom. 12, 1.

II

THE EARLY CHRISTIANS AND THE TEMPLE

In the first of his idealizing summaries, Luke says of the Christian community in Jerusalem that "day by day, attending the temple together, and breaking bread in their homes, they partook of food with glad and generous hearts, praising God and having favor with all the people".[7] It was probably this post-Pentecostal period Luke had in mind when in his gospel (24, 53) he says that after the ascension the disciples "returned to Jerusalem with great joy, and were continually in the temple blessing God". The opening chapters of Acts show us how much the temple was part of the early days of the Church. Peter and John go up there at the hour of prayer, the ninth hour.[8] They and the other apostles preach Jesus in the temple area. Their favorite meeting place there seems to have been Solomon's portico.[9]

In this attachment to the temple the early Church had Christ's example. He taught there as a boy [10] and often later during his public ministry.[11] Lack of respect for his Father's house aroused him to anger.[12] He forbade the carrying of loads through the temple area.[13] He did not condemn the apostles for their pride in the magnificence of the temple structure.[14] In fact, he wept over the sad fate soon to befall it.[15] Paul, too, despite his teaching on the universality of Christ's religion, was attached to the temple and went there to pray.[16]

The ninth hour—i.e., 3 P.M.—at which Peter and John went

[7] Acts 2, 46f.
[8] Acts 3, 1.
[9] Acts 3, 11; 5, 12.
[10] Lk. 2, 46.
[11] Mk. 11, 11. 27; 12, 35; 14, 49 and par.; Jn. 2, 14; 5, 14; 7, 14. 28; 8, 24; 10, 23; 11, 56; 18, 20.
[12] Mk. 11, 15 and par.; Jn. 2, 14.
[13] Mk. 11, 16.
[14] Mk. 13, 1 and par.
[15] Mk. 13, 2 and par.; Mt. 23, 37.
[16] Acts 22, 17; 21, 23-25.

to the temple (Acts 13, 1) was by New Testament times the hour of the evening sacrifice,[17] the *Tamid* or perpetual sacrifice.[18] This daily whole-burnt offering was the most important part of the regular worship of the sanctuary, and one to which the Israelites were devotedly attached.[19] Its suppression was the greatest of disasters.[20] Outside the temple the ninth hour was an hour of prayer for Jews and God-fearing pagans.[21]

The Christian community probably united with Israel in prayer. Sacrifice they scarcely offered. Yet, despite their attachment to the temple they were separated from official Judaism through belief in the resurrection. The risen Savior, not the temple, was the center of their lives. They were united among themselves, and as a group stood aloof from the other Jews, and were considered by these as a body apart.[22] Their choice of the portico of Solomon as their favorite meeting place [23] may have had a special reason. Jesus had taught there. It was there that the Jewish religious leaders asked him to tell them openly if he was the Christ.[24] This is what the apostles were now proclaiming publicly.

This close attachment to the temple lasted probably to the martyrdom of Stephen, some seven years or so. During these years the preaching and teaching of the young Church in the templo [25] must have been inspired by Christ's teaching on himself as the true Temple.[26] Only after the resurrection did they really understand it: "When therefore he was raised from the dead, his disciples remembered that he had said this; and they

[17] Cf. Josephus, *Ant.* 14, 4, 3.

[18] On this, see E. Schürer, *A History of the Jewish People in the Time of Jesus Christ* (Edinburgh, 1901), pp. 284-89.

[19] Ex. 29, 38-42; Num. 28, 38.

[20] Cf. Dan. 8. 11-15; 11. 31; Josephus, *Ant.* 14, 4, 3.

[21] Cf. Acts 10, 3. 30. On the Jewish hours of prayer see Schürer *op. cit.*, pp. 290f., note 248; G. F. Moore, *Judaism* II, pp. 219f.; see also D. Y. Hadidian in *Theol. Studies* 25 (1964), pp. 59-69.

[22] Cf. Acts 5, 13.

[23] Acts 3, 3. 11; 5, 12.

[24] Jn. 10, 23.

[25] Acts 5, 42.

[26] Jn. 2, 19; Mk. 14, 58 and par.; cf. Mk. 15, 29; Mt. 27, 63. See further Y. Congar, *The Mystery of the Temple* (London, 1962).

believed in the Scripture and the Word which Jesus had spoken"
(Jn. 2, 22). It was probably during this period that the theology
of the Christian community as the true temple of God was
formed.[27] The sacrifice of the passover lamb had no further
meaning for Christians. The true passover Lamb, Christ, had
already been sacrificed.[28] Neither had the sacrifice of the lamb
of the *Tamid* offering, which was most probably then considered
expiatory by the Jews.[29] The Christian Church had its own
Tamid offering, offered through Christ Jesus: "Through him let
us *continually* offer up a sacrifice of prayer to God, the fruit of
lips that acknowledge his name" (Heb. 13, 15).

III
WORSHIP IN PRIVATE HOUSES

The Jerusalem community attended the temple daily and
broke bread at home (*kat'oikon*).[30] Inasmuch as the continuation of the verse tells us that the community partook of food
with glad and generous hearts, we can scarcely take *kat'oikon* to
mean that each broke bread in his own home. The author of Acts
is thinking of assemblies in private houses, in contradistinction to
their meetings in the temple area. In the breaking of bread the
Christian community had a rite which set it apart from Judaism.
It was something which could not be done in the temple. Teaching was also part of these assemblies in private houses.[31] This
included "the teaching of the apostles" (Acts 2, 42) which would

[27] Cf. 1 Pet. 2, 4-6; 1 Cor. 3, 16; 6, 19; 2 Cor. 5, 1-15; 1 Tim. 3,
15; Eph. 2, 19-23.
[28] 1 Cor. 5, 7.
[29] Almost all sacrifice was considered expiatory in Judaism by the
New Testament period. The Targum of Pseudo-Jonathan (Num. 28,
38) says that the morning and evening lambs of the *Tamid* offering
were sacrificed to atone for the sins of the night and of the day. Cf.
further G. Vermes, *Scripture and Tradition in Judaism* (Leiden, 1961),
pp. 192-227.
[30] Acts 2, 46.
[31] Acts 5, 42.

in turn embrace the words and deeds of Jesus as these referred to the life of the community. These house-assemblies were also places of prayer.[32]

The constant elements of these assemblies seem to have been the teaching by the apostles, the breaking of bread and prayer.[33] These three must also have generally gone together in Christian liturgical assemblies outside of Jerusalem and Palestine.

There were probably at Jerusalem a number of such houses at which sections of the community came together. The increasing numbers of believers would require this.[34] They were, naturally, houses offered for this purpose by believers. One such house is known to us. It is that of Mary, the mother of John Mark (Acts 12, 12). This must have been a well known meeting place for the Christians of Jerusalem. It was probably the house in which Christ ate the Last Supper with his disciples, the one in which he appeared to them after the resurrection,[35] and that in which his followers were gathered at Pentecost. Tradition locates it on Mount Sion, where the basilica *Sancta Sion Mater Omnium Ecclesiarum* was later erected.

Outside of Jerusalem the first Christian assemblies were also held in private houses. The house of Simon the Tanner of Joppe [36] was probably one of these, and so possibly was that of Ananias at Damascus.[37] The house where the prophets and teachers at Antioch "worshiped the Lord and fasted" [38] may have been another. The house of Lydia, the slave convert of Philippi, was probably the place where Paul met his fellow Christians and exhorted them.[39] The house of Jason at Thessalonica [40] was probably used for assemblies in that city. Aquila and Prisca had

[32] Cf. Acts 4, 23. 30; 12, 5. 12.
[33] Cf. Acts 2, 42.
[34] Cf. Acts 2, 47; 4, 4; 5, 14; 6, 7.
[35] Lk. 24, 33; Jn. 20, 19-26.
[36] Acts 9, 43; 10, 9.
[37] Acts 9, 10f. 19.
[38] Acts 13, 1f.
[39] Acts 16, 15. 40.
[40] Acts 17, 5-9; cf. Rom. 16, 21.

given over their house at Ephesus for Christian assemblies; Paul speaks of the Church that is in their house.[41] At Colossae the Church assembled in the house of Philemon.[42] At Laodicea the center was the house of Nympha.[43] The upper room, on the third floor, at which the brethren assembled at Troas [44] most probably belonged to a member of the Christian community.

At Corinth the first assemblies were probably held in the house of Stephanas,[45] but there were also assemblies in the house of Gaius.[46] Our fullest information on early Christian assemblies comes from Corinth, and this is due to the fact that Paul finds much to remedy there.[47] In this city there were in fact two distinct forms of Christian assembly.[48] One was for the celebration of the Lord's supper,[49] to which only believers would be admitted. The other was a general assembly for prayers, hymns, exhortations, etc.[50] At these latter assemblies the gifts of the Spirit were very much in evidence. Interested non-believers could attend.[51] What exact relation one assembly bore to the other and whether they coincided we cannot say.

IV
LITURGY AND APOSTOLIC AUTHORITY

The liturgical assemblies of Jerusalem were intimately connected with the apostles and their teaching.[52] From 1 Corin-

[41] 1 Cor. 16, 19.
[42] Philem. 2.
[43] Col. 4, 15.
[44] Acts 20, 7-12. That the Christian community of Troas and not merely the traveling companions of Paul were present is indicated by the context.
[45] Cf. 1 Cor. 16, 15f.; cf. 1 Cor. 1, 16.
[46] Cf. Rom. 16, 23.
[47] Cf. 1 Cor. 10, 10-14.
[48] Cf. M. Goguel, *L'Église Primitive*, pp. 274-81; E. B. Allo, *Première Épitre aux Corinthians* (Paris, 1956), pp. 285-316, 384-86.
[49] 1 Cor. 11, 17-33.
[50] 1 Cor. 14.
[51] 1 Cor. 14, 22-25.
[52] Cf. Acts 2, 42.

thians we know that Paul considered public worship something very much under apostolic control and that he had laid down certain principles which held for all the churches he had founded. This comes from the very nature of the liturgy. Since *lex credendi* is *lex orandi,* worship must express revealed doctrine. It was for the apostles to determine when it did not. They had the task of distinguishing false manifestations of piety from the true. "No one speaking by the Spirit says Jesus is cursed." [53] Where public worship touches immediately on revealed doctrine, as in the Lord's supper, both the apostles and other Christians were bound by the tradition they had received from the Lord.

But apart from dogmatic considerations, Paul had to see to it that the liturgy fulfilled its purpose of building up the Church. Practice had to be consonant with belief and be such that believers and outsiders were edified by it. "God is not the God of confusion but of peace." [54]

Paul left the Corinthians in no doubt about his authority to give directives for religious assemblies. He commended them on certain matters where they had maintained the traditions that he had delivered to them.[55] The matter in question is the deportment of women at public worship. He permits no deviation from the practice he has laid down for all his churches.[56] "If anyone is disposed to be contentious, we recognize no other practice, nor do the churches of God" (1 Cor. 11, 16). He cannot approve of them on their manner of celebrating the eucharist (1 Cor. 11, 17). He gives instructions on the use of the gifts conferred on them by the Spirit (Chapter 14), ending with an injunction that women remain silent in church—as apparently was his ruling for all the churches founded by him. Recalling the universal practice, he ends with the words: "What! Did the Word of God originate with you, or are you the only ones it has reached?" (1 Cor. 14, 37).

The idea is that Corinth, being part of the universal Church,

[53] 1 Cor. 12, 3.
[54] 1 Cor. 14, 33.
[55] 1 Cor. 11, 2.
[56] Cf. 1 Cor. 4, 17; 7, 17.

cannot deviate at will in liturgical practice. What follows from all this is that the Pauline churches appear to have been governed in liturgical matters by certain principles from which the apostle will allow no deviation. The elders he appointed in his churches [57] would have had the task of seeing that his wishes were carried out. His liturgical tradition would have been basically that of the Jerusalem community, from which the Word of the Lord came to Corinth.[58]

Certain general principles apart, however, there must have been quite a variety within the Pauline churches, a variety stemming from circumstances, but particularly from the activity of the Holy Spirit which Paul certainly would have done nothing to stifle.[59]

V

DETAILS OF CHRISTIAN WORSHIP

The Lord's Day [60]

The available evidence indicates that at a very early date the first day of the week, the Lord's day,[61] had become a sacred day for Christians, one in which they came together in honor of the resurrection [62] and to celebrate the liturgy. That the custom was already established by 57 A.D. in the Pauline churches we can gather from 1 Cor. 16, 1f. where he directs that on that day a collection be taken up in Corinth for the Church in Jerusalem. In the same text he tells them that he has reminded the Galatian Church to do likewise. At passover of the following year Paul breaks bread with the brethren at Troas on the first day of the week.[63] This might be because he had to depart next day. The manner in which Luke mentions this particular day in connec-

---

[57] Cf. Acts 14, 23; 20, 17.

[58] Cf. Is. 2, 3.

[59] Cf. 1 Thess. 5, 19.

[60] Cf. J. A. Jungmann, *The Early Liturgy to the Time of Gregory the Great* (London, 1960), pp. 19-25.

[61] Apoc. 1, 10.

[62] Mt. 28, 1; Mk. 16, 2; Lk. 24, 1; Jn. 20, 1. 9.

[63] Acts 20, 7.

tion with the breaking of bread, however, leads one to believe that it was an established custom for Christians to assemble for the eucharist on that day. We can presume that the Lord's day was also honored in Jerusalem. The Sabbath rest, however, continued to be observed by Jewish Christians.[64]

The Feast of Easter [65]

It is uncertain whether in Paul's day, or in apostolic times, the Church celebrated an annual feast in honor of the resurrection on the occurrence of the Jewish passover or at some other time.[66] Certainly, a text such as Galatians 4, 9f. creates no difficulty against such a feast, as what Paul there condemns are feasts connected with the danger of apostasy. The text of 1 Corinthians 5, 6-8 at first sight seems to presuppose the celebration of the passover (the Christian Easter, naturally) at Corinth. Yet, this text can scarcely be pressed. The imagery used may be due to the symbolism of the passover in Paul's mind, rather than the celebration of a Christian passover at Corinth. Paul can write from the abundance of his Hebrew heart and express himself in Jewish liturgical symbolic language even to Gentile Christians. In 2 Corinthians 3, 7—4, 6 we have a good example.[67] Paul follows the Jewish calender, dating events by the feasts of Pentecost [68] and of Unleavened Bread.[69] Yet, these were then scarcely feasts of the Christian Church.

The Lord's Supper and the Breaking of Bread [70]

The very name it bears (deipnon) shows that, at least at Corinth, the eucharist was celebrated in the evening. At Corinth

[64] Cf. Mt. 24, 20.

[65] Cf. J. Jeremias, "Pascha," in Theol. Wört. zum. N.T. 5 (1954), pp. 894-903.

[66] Cf. Allo, op. cit., pp. 126f.; H. Schürmann, "Die Anfänge Christlicher Osterfeier," in Theol. Quartalschrift 131 (1951), pp. 414-25; J. Delorme, "The Last Supper and the Pasch in the N.T.," in The Eucharist in the N.T. (cf. below, note 70), pp. 26f.; J. Jeremias, op. cit. p. 900, note 44.

[67] Cf. M. McNamara, op. cit. (note 4 above), pp. 166-88.

[68] 1 Cor. 16, 8; Acts 20, 16.

[69] Acts 20, 6.

[70] Cf. The Eucharist in the N.T. ed. J. Delorme (London, 1964).

it was combined with a full meal, which was originally intended as a sign of brotherhood, an *agape*. At Corinth, instead of being the sacrament of unity,[71] abuses had turned it into a cause of disunion.[72] The celebration included the account of the consecration, a tradition which Paul says he had received "from the Lord" (1 Corinthians 11, 23). He probably got it "from the Lord" through the Church at Jerusalem. The very words he uses ("received" and "handed on") are technical terms in Judaism for the transmission of tradition.[73]

We must look on the *breaking of bread* by Paul and the brethren at Troas (Acts 20, 7. 11) as the Lord's supper, the eucharist. On that particular occasion the bread was actually broken after midnight. The breaking of bread among the Christians of Jerusalem (Acts 2, 42. 46) was also probably the eucharist. Luke, at any rate, appears to have understood it in this sense. From the expression itself one could not conclude this, of course. The blessing (*berachah*) and breaking of bread were merely the Jewish grace before meals. A pious Jew did not eat without first blessing and breaking the bread. It is in this sense of grace before meals that the words are to be understood in Acts 27, 35. However, since the Jerusalem community must have celebrated the eucharist, we can legitimately see reference to it in the breaking of bread of Acts 2, 42. 46. From one action connected with the rite, the Lord's supper was called "the breaking of bread". Another of the actions (*berachah*, "blessing" or "thanksgiving": *Eucharistia*) gave it another name.

Instruction

Teaching (*didache*), instruction in the faith, was an important function in the religious assemblies of the early Church. For the community at Jerusalem we have the evidence of Acts.[74] We are given no details on what form this instruction took. It would

---

[71] 1 Cor. 10, 17.
[72] 1 Cor. 11, 17-33.
[73] Cf. Mishnah, *Aboth* 1, 1.
[74] Acts 2, 42; 11, 26.

doubtless be on the life and teaching of Christ and the application of these to Christian living. Instruction, exhortation, etc. were also regular at the assemblies of Corinth.[75] They were prophetic gifts. Paul's instructions must have been lengthy. At Troas this was certainly so (Acts 20, 7-12). He spoke on until midnight, broke bread and ate, and then carried on talking (*homilesas*), with the community present until daybreak. *Homileo* (whence our "homily"; cf. *sermo*—"sermon") of this text means "to carry on a conversation". It was a dialogue rather than a sermon. Questions were asked and Paul answered. From 1 Corinthians 14, 34f. we gather that questions must have been a regular feature of the assemblies at Corinth. This practice may be reflected in some of Paul's letters where a fictitious interlocutor is made to pose objections. The quality of the sermons and discourses must have varied with the circumstances. There would undoubtedly be appropriate compositions for special occasions, such as the conferring of baptism. Some exegetes see such a baptismal homily behind the first epistle of Peter.

Prayer [76]

Above all else, the early Christians came together for public prayer,[77] a prayer in which they were conscious of their union with the universal Church.[78] Acts 4, 24-30 gives us an example of the prayer of the Jerusalem community. The most noticeable feature of this prayer is its spontaneity. There were as yet scarcely any fixed formulae. Judaism had formal prayers, yet it knew the value of extemporizing in prayer and commended it. The Jewish order of prayer during the first two centuries of our era, notes G. F. Moore,[79] "was a directory rather than a formulary. It was not only licit but commendable for the in-

---

[75] 1 Cor. 14, 3-7, 19, 24f.

[76] Fr. J. M. Nielen, *Gebet und Gottesdienst im N.T.* (Freiburg im B., 1937).

[77] Cf. Acts 1, 14; 2, 42; 6, 4; 12, 5; 16, 16; Rom. 12, 12; 15, 30; Phil. 4, 6; 1 Tim. 2, 1; 5, 5; etc.

[78] Cf. Acts 12, 5; Rom. 2, 1; 5, 5; etc.

[79] *Judaism* II, p. 227.

dividual to vary the phraseology and extemporize upon its themes". Even with prayers coming basically from Christ, the early Christians could take liberties, reproducing the essentials in varying formulae. The *ipsissima verba Jesu* was not a preoccupation of the early Church. This we can see from the different forms of the *Pater Noster* and of the words of consecration.

At times *fasting* was joined with prayer [80] in the true biblical and Jewish tradition and in accord with the words of Christ.[81]

Occasionally *private prayer* was *directed to Christ* (cf. Acts 7, 59). *The communal prayer* of Christians, however, *was directed to God the Father,* to whom the community prayed in the name of Jesus, or through the Lord Jesus Christ,[82] Christ being mediator between God and man.[83]

The congregation united themselves with the prayers recited publicly by answering "Amen".[84] This response the Church took over from the liturgy of the Old Testament period through the synagogue.

Hymns [85]

The influence of the Holy Spirit manifested itself in the liturgical assemblies, among other ways, in the impromptu utterances of sacred song.[86] These liturgical compositions are referred to as psalms [87] or hymns.[88] We have examples of such impromptu compositions in the Old Testament, and the Jews of the apostolic age had their own hymnic compositions (Qumran, the Aramaic Targums). Some of these liturgical songs have very probably found their way into the New Testament. The *Magnificat,*

---

[80] Acts 13, 3; 14, 23; 1 Cor. 7, 5.
[81] Cf. Mk. 2, 20; etc.
[82] Heb. 13, 13f.; Rom. 1, 8; Jude 25.
[83] Cf. J. Jungmann, *The Place of Christ in Liturgical Prayer* (London-Dublin, 1965), pp. 127-43.
[84] 1 Cor. 14, 16; 2 Cor. 1, 20.
[85] Cf. G. Delling, "Hymnos . . . Psalmos," in *Theol. Wört. zum N.T.* 8 (1967), pp. 492-506.
[86] 1 Cor. 14, 15. 26.
[87] 1 Cor. 14, 26; Eph. 5, 19; Jas. 5, 13.
[88] Col. 3, 16; Eph. 5, 19.

Benedictus and *Nunc Dimittis* may have originated in the liturgy of Jerusalem. We have clearer examples of liturgical hymns, or fragments of them, in the New Testament.[89] These examples deal with the eternal existence of Christ, his incarnation and glorification and his salvific work in the Church.

Public Reading of the Scriptures

Timothy is expected to attend "to the reading (*anagnosis*), to preaching, and to teaching" (1 Tim. 4, 13). The RSV and the *New English Bible* correctly paraphrase the first word as "the public reading of Scripture". The writings of Paul were read in the public assemblies,[90] and these were probably reckoned as Scripture when 1 Timothy was composed.[91] Yet the Scriptures referred to in the passage of 1 Timothy probably are principally, if not solely, the writing of the Old Testament with which Timothy was familiar.[92] In this the church of Ephesus would have taken over a practice from the synagogue. St. Paul presupposes such an acquaintance with the Old Testament on the part of his readers that one may legitimately presume that the synagogue custom was taken over by the communities founded by Paul and perhaps in other churches as well.

VI

WORSHIP IN THE SYNAGOGUE
IN NEW TESTAMENT TIMES [93]

By New Testament times the synagogue played a central role in Judaism, both in Palestine and in the diaspora. The constant parts of the synagogue service were prayer, Scripture and, where

---

[89] Eph. 5, 13; 1 Tim. 3, 16; Col. 1, 15-20; 1 Pet. 2, 21-25; perhaps Phil. 2, 6-11.

[90] Cf. 1 Thess. 5, 27; Col. 4, 16; cf. Apoc. 1, 3.

[91] Cf. 2 Pet. 3, 16.

[92] Cf. 2 Tim. 3, 15.

[93] Cf. E. Schürer, *op. cit.*, pp. 75-89; G. F. Moore, *Judaism* I, pp. 291-307.

possible, a homily. The service opened with the *Shema* ("Hear, O Israel": Deut. 6, 4f.), Israel's profession of faith. This was followed by the prayer proper, the *Tephillah,* a series of benedictions which became codified toward the end of the 1st century and is known as the *Shemoneh Esreh*—i.e., the Eighteen (Benedictions). Next came a reading from the Pentateuch, followed by one from the Prophets (*the Haftarah*). In Palestine both were read in Hebrew and accompanied by a rendering into Aramaic (known as a *Targum*).[94] In the 1st century there was no *lectio continua* of the prophets. The choice of text was left to the reader (cf. Lk. 4, 17) or to the head of the synagogue. In Palestine, at any rate, a *lectio continua* of the Pentateuch seems to have been obligatory in theory, even if not always adhered to in practice. By the 3rd century, Palestine had a *triennial cycle* for the reading of the Pentateuch, the *lectio continua* being completed in the course of three years. This triennial cycle is not attested in earlier sources. It seems to have been unknown to 2nd-century rabbis.[95] Some authors favor a seven-year cycle for the earlier period, others an annual cycle, others still a cycle lasting three and a half years.[96] Probably, with the proviso that the Pentateuch be read consecutively from Genesis to Deuteronomy, the actual manner in which this was done was left to local custom. Theories (and there are a number of them) based on a given fixed cycle of Scripture reading for Palestine in New Testament times must then be viewed with due reserve.

The homily [97] on the Scripture passage read was a most important part of the service. A member of the congregation or a visiting Jew could be invited to give it (cf. Lk. 4, 17-21; Acts 13, 15-41). This ended in Palestine with a prayer blessing the divine name. This in the course of time developed into the prayer known as the *Kaddish,*[98] which also came to be used in other

[94] On these, cf. McNamara, *op. cit.,* pp. 38-45; R. Le Déaut, *Introduction a la littérature targumique* I (Rome, 1966).

[95] McNamara, *op cit.,* pp. 42-45.

[96] Cf. Le Déaut, *op. cit.,* pp. 45-51.

[97] See M. Maher, M.S.C., "Reflections on Jewish and Christian Preaching," in *Irish Eccles. Record* 108 (1967), pp. 227-42.

[98] Cf. David de Sola Pool, *The Old Jewish-Aramaic Prayer, the Kad-*

parts of the synagogue service. It bears some remarkable similarities with the *Pater Noster.*

VII
ORIGINALITY OF CHRISTIAN WORSHIP

The public worship of the *traditional Greek gods* was still very much alive in apostolic times.[99] No comparison can really be made between early Christian liturgy and what little we know of the actual worship of these cults. For Paul, pagan "gods" were demons; to sacrifice to them was to sacrifice to demons (1 Cor. 10, 14-22). The failure of traditional religion to satisfy the religious longings of the masses had by New Testament times led to a revival of interest in ancient Greek *mystery religions* [100] and to the introduction of others from Egypt and the East. The golden age of these religions came only later (3rd century A.D.). Our knowledge of the ritual of these cults is minimal, due among other things to the law binding the initiates to secrecy. Lack of certain information on the position of these mystery cults during the New Testament period renders any comparison between them and Christian liturgy difficult. The day when Christianity was considered by some scholars to descend genetically from them has, however, long since passed. Christianity and its early liturgy differ totally from them in the fact that the former are concerned with historical events, the death and resurrection of Jesus Christ *sub Pontio Pilato,* while the latter are basically nature religions.

Christian liturgy differs from Jewish liturgy in the same way as Christianity differs from Judaism. The *Shema,* "The Lord our

dish (1909). Text in Jewish prayerbooks, in F. E. Warren, *The Liturgy and Ritual of the Ante-Nicene Church* (London, 1897), pp. 214f., and in J. Bonsirven, *Textes Rabbiniques,* p. 3.

[99] Cf. Acts 14, 8-18; 19, 23-41; 1 Cor. 10, 14-22. For Hellenistic Religion, cf. R. H. Pfeiffer, *History of N.T. Times* (New York, 1949), pp. 127-65.

[100] On these see H. Rahner, *Greek Myths and Christian Mystery* (London, 1963), Chapter 1; Pfeiffer, *loc. cit.*

God is one Lord", was the Jewish profession of faith; that of Christians was "Jesus is Lord". Christians worshiped one true God, but *through Christ Jesus*. Their worship is centered around Christ. The hymnic compositions proper to their liturgy are on Christ. After the example of Christ they addressed God as "Abba, Father"—a form of prayer unknown to Judaism. That Jewish worship influenced the liturgy and literature of the New Testament seems certain, even though it is often difficult to prove that any particular Christian rite is due to the practice of the synagogue. Jewish liturgy was a most genuine expression of Jewish faith. As the New Testament took to itself the Old and fulfilled it, so would it naturally do with themes from Jewish liturgy, adopting and transposing them to its own life and teaching.

Hans Meyer, S.J./*Innsbruck, Austria*

How Much Change Is Permissible in the Liturgy?

As liturgical reform proceeds apace, many people are asking these questions: Are we justified in replacing traditional, time-honored rites with new, untested forms of worship? How far can we legitimately go in shaping older liturgical forms to suit our present-day outlook? What elements in the Christian liturgy are unchangeable? What elements must be preserved to guarantee its legitimacy? As time goes on, these questions will assume greater urgency, and we therefore shall try to provide some tentative answers in this article.

I
WHAT IS LITURGICAL WORSHIP?

A Grace Formally Instituted by God

Liturgy, as we understand it here, is an encounter between God and man that is embodied in words, elements and gestures. It is man's communion with God, gratuitously offered by God to man in the saving community of the Church and under sacramental signs. In the liturgical worship of the Church, the salvation community of the new covenant that was founded by Christ, the individual is blessed and sanctified by God; in return, he has a chance to direct his thanks, his petitions and his sacrifice to God.

This worship takes concrete shape in the liturgical assembly of the local community, which represents the whole Church. It is carried out in the celebration of the eucharist, in the administration and reception of the sacraments, in the recitation of the Divine Office, in sacramental services and in other forms of divine worship.[1]

The core of such worship is encounter and community between God and man. On one side, God offers himself to man; he grants salvation—that is, a participation in his own perfect life. On the other side, man serves and honors God by accepting this divine life, making it his own, and surrendering himself to God as a member of the ecclesial community.[2]

The history of religions bears abundant testimony to the fact that divine worship is seen essentially as a *grace* that is *formally instituted by God.*[3] Man can only approach God if God summons him. God himself must let man know when, where and how men may encounter him; man cannot determine the time, place and manner on his own. Man cannot force this community with God any more than he can force other love relationships.

To accept love and reciprocate love is a free gift. If this is true of interhuman relationships, how much more true it is of the God-man relationship. God himself must speak the first word; he must call man to himself. Any and every attempt to force God into contact with an individual or a people is magic, not liturgy.

Thus liturgy is a formally instituted grace. This is the real and most compelling reason why liturgy involves an *obligation* that finds expression and perdurance in tradition and summons man to obedience.

A Human Action

Liturgical worship is essentially a *human* action as well; therefore, it is *historical,* just as man himself is. Liturgy has a symbolic quality, varying with time and place, that can be grasped here

[1] *Constitution on the Sacred Liturgy,* nn. 12-13.

[2] *Ibid.,* nn. 5-13.

[3] M. Eliade, *The Sacred and the Profane,* particularly the chapters on sacred times and sacred places.

and now.[4] Among its symbolic features is the shape of the Church in a given epoch: her offices and rites reflect the historical experience of men and their varying cultures.

When God enters into a relationship with man, this community between creator and creature cannot be realized in a framework of transcendent other-worldliness. It is tied up with the created order established by God, and with its concomitant features of time and place. In a word, it is tied up with history, where the community between God and man grows and reaches fulfillment as salvation history.

The historical cast of all created life provides the basic justification for legitimate liturgical *change*, and such change is found in the cultic worship of the old and new covenants.[5] Individuals, culture groups and the human species as a whole find fulfillment in an historical process of individual and collective development. In a living process that spans the moments of time, they gradually attain self-awareness and self-fulfillment. Between childhood and maturity lies a process of individual becoming that is characterized by change. The human species, too, follows a path that can be seen as a progressive movement; by stages it moves somewhat closer to the fulfillment that it can attain within the limits of the world.

It is evident, then, that man's worship of God *must* change if it is to remain an adequate expression of his individual or collective life. It would hardly be appropriate for a child to worship God in the same way as an adult. In like manner, the Church of today could not adequately worship God in the same way as the primitive Church. To do this would be to ignore the self-awareness, the insights and the experiences she has accumulated over the course of her growth in history. How could we deny to the Church the right and the necessity of growth and development, when we recognize and try to foster these things in the life of the individual and in the course of secular history?

[4] See A. Verheul, *Einführung in die Liturgie* (Vienna, 1964), pp. 155f.; M. Löhrer, "Kulttheologie und Liturgie der Kirche," in *HPTh* I (Freiburg/Breisgau, 1964), p. 307.
[5] Th. Klauser, *Kleine abendländische Liturgiegeschichte* (Bonn, 1965).

An Ecclesial Action

It is simply impossible for us to overlook the fact that the Church, too, is involved in a process of growth and development and that she is thereby gradually moving closer to her definitive fulfillment.

In olden times, St. Patrick made 300 genuflections every day, and others bowed their head to the ground thousands of times.[6] These practices may seem rather superficial and external to us now, but they undoubtedly corresponded to an inner ideal *in their day,* even though they could not be regarded as obligatory. To regard them as obligatory for every stage of the Church's development would be to miss the point entirely.

If this is true for personal ascetical practices, it is also true for the liturgical worship of the Church. It necessarily takes on ever new overtones from the pious life of the individual and the community. It sprouts from their intellectual and practical appreciation of the faith, which is not the same today as it was in the early days of the Church.

To sum up, let us recall once again that liturgical worship is not left to the whim of man. It is a grace of divine institution. At the same time, it is made concrete within history, where God and man encounter each other and enact salvation history. This means that worship of God is subject to change—change which is willed by God, approved by him and guided by his Spirit. The measuring rod is not God's immutability but the historicity of man in the world created by God.

II

LITURGY AND SALVATION HISTORY

Theologically speaking, both the maintenance of liturgical traditions and liturgical reform find their justification in the per-

[6] O. Zimmermann, *Lehrbuch der Aszetik* (Freiburg/Breisgau, ²1932), p. 353.

son of Jesus Christ and the salvation history which centers around him. In Jesus Christ, God himself entered the world and its history; thus, in Christ, God and the world come together without being fused together indistinguishably. The immutable majesty of God meets the created world that is striving toward fulfillment in history. As the accomplishment of Christ's priestly work in history (*Constitution on the Sacred Liturgy,* n. 7), the Church's liturgical worship participates in the mystery of the God-Man and derives its life from him alone.[7]

In Jesus Christ, God entered history in a specific epoch with its own concrete circumstances; his purpose was to establish a new community between himself and mankind. In like manner, the forms of encounter between God and man in the old covenant were also marked by the historical situation in which they arose. Jesus did not criticize the legitimate kernel of authenticity in the Old Testament liturgy established by God; he himself, for example, took part in the temple services. Jesus' criticism was directed against the decadent and outmoded forms that would freeze the liturgy in a false traditionalism. Some people wanted the liturgy to be a fixed and ready-made tool for forcing God to look favorably on man, and this was what Christ opposed.

Since liturgical worship was meant to be a *personal* activity, God left it open to his summons in history and subject to change. Jesus took issue with any and every attempt to falsify the existing liturgy and to distort its true nature, for it was merely a type of promise of the perfect liturgy embodied in himself.[8] Because the leaders of the chosen people tried to turn the liturgy into a safe, immutable possession, one which would give them a quasi-legal claim on God, the liturgy of the temple was confronted with an awesome crisis. The temple was destroyed and the chosen people dispersed because they had not accepted the change from type to perfected reality.

[7] The symbolic character of the liturgy is grounded in the person and life of Jesus himself, who is "the image of the invisible God" (Col. 1, 15). See G. Deussen, *Die neue liturgische Gemeinde* (Frankfurt/M., 1968), p. 16. The incarnational structure of the liturgy is also brought out by C. Vagaggini, *Il senso teologico della liturgica* ([2]1957).

The books of the New Testament and the practice of the primitive Church indicate that the relationship between the youthful Church and the Old Testament temple was affected by a growing realization of this situation. At first Christians participated in the Old Testament liturgy. They made a clean break with their Judaic heritage only when Judaism rejected Christ, branding him the subverter of the old covenant and its liturgy instead of its perfecter. This Judaic attitude found clear expression in the persecutions that were waged against the nascent Christian community.

The evangelist Mark saw God's kingdom breaking into the world with the coming of Christ, and he looked forward to the immediate fulfillment of the old covenant and its promises. In Luke's writings, however, we already see the internal growth of the community; as time goes on, it moves away from the old covenant and begins to spread throughout the world. Paul gives us some idea as to why this was necessary. He began by preaching in the synagogue and participating in its liturgy. But as he began to encounter rejection there—that is, rejection of Christ as the fulfillment of the covenant—he began to preach him to the community in a new way. Christ was now the Lord of the Church, who is operative in her and with her through the Holy Spirit. In Acts, Luke offers an explanation for the separation of Christianity from Judaism, which was by now pretty well complete. Under the guidance of the Holy Spirit, the risen Lord had expanded into his Church.[9]

---

[8] See Mk. 13, 1f. Jesus follows the tradition of the Old Testament prophets in his selective criticism of the temple. From Isaiah to Jeremiah there is a clear line of development. Isaiah still regards Sion as the center to which all must come if they are to attain salvation. Jeremiah already perceives that the temple can go by the boards, that it is only secondary at best; for him, the decisive things are the covenant and the word which supports it (Jer. 7, 22f.).

[9] See the exegetical works on the writings of Luke—in particular, H. Conzelmann, *Die Mitte der Zeit: Studien zur Theologie des Lukas* (Tübingen, 1954).

III
THE EPOCH OF THE CHURCH

The basic framework of liturgical life that took shape from these developments has general validity *for the whole new covenant*, and hence for the entire epoch of the Church. On the one hand, man's encounter with God hinges around the definitive revelation in Jesus Christ; man cannot manipulate his liturgical worship at will. On the other hand, man must be ever ready to allow change into this liturgy, because the Church is the perduring presence of Christ in history.

In the Church, Jesus is made present in this world as the *living Christ*; in her, he moves through the centuries. Isn't it more likely that the Lord would appear to us today as one of our contemporaries, rather than as a relic of a bygone age?

Only in Christ can we find community with God. This is true today and forever. Thus in the Church there is a legitimate liturgical worship that was instituted by Christ and is not subject to man's whim. It is man's *real possibility* of encountering God in an authentic way. But the Church does not stand still in time, like a rock in the middle of the sea; she, too, has a history. She is, in fact, the principle of history. She is the leaven in the history of mankind, and her task is to move this history forward toward its fulfillment.

Church history in general, and the history of the liturgy in particular, clearly show that there has been constant change in Christian teaching, Christian ways of living and Christian liturgical worship. This process is essentially legitimate and necessary. If this legitimate process of change had not taken place, we would not have the developed tradition we do possess today. Neither the Church as a whole nor the individual Christian has the right to hinder this divinely willed process of change by misguided attempts at petrification.

Contrary to the false impression that is often created, the

Church is not just the guardian of a finished kingdom. She is also the vanguard in man's march toward total fulfillment. This fulfillment does not lie on the other side of the temporal world; it is a fulfillment in the created order, because God has definitively entered the world in Jesus Christ.

IV
CHANGEABLE AND UNCHANGEABLE
ELEMENTS IN THE LITURGY

Now we can ask ourselves the critical question: What is changeable in the liturgy and what is not changeable? To begin with, its character *as an institution* is not changeable. In other words, we cannot change the fact that our community with God, gratuitously offered to us in Christ and his Church, must be accepted in accordance with the law laid down by God.

For this reason, liturgy is also essentially *bound up with a tradition*. It is tied up with its historical roots and beginnings in the person of Jesus Christ, who instituted it, and we cannot give this up.

Moreover, our liturgy necessarily has *a communal character*. It is the cultic worship of God's covenant people. Joined together in a visible community and united with their head, Jesus Christ, they render present his person and his salvation through the power of the Holy Spirit. Salvation and the worship which dispenses it are necessarily communal because "God did not choose to save and sanctify men one by one, excluding any mutual interconnection; rather, he chose to establish them as a people who would acknowledge him in truth and serve him in holiness".[10]

Finally, this liturgical worship will always be carried out *with visible signs*. It must be inserted into our world in such a way that its words and actions can be experienced as a fully human activity by the faithful.

[10] *Dogmatic Constitution on the Church*, n. 9; cf. Deussen, *op. cit.*, p. 60.

Substantive and Material Elements

The substantive and material elements of the liturgy, however, are not unchangeable of necessity. Here we must distinguish various elements which have differing degrees of obligatory character by virtue of the institutional and traditional character of the liturgy. There are some signs—i.e., words, elements and gestures—that were used by Christ himself and bequeathed to the Church. Other liturgical traditions arose in the Church and were sanctioned by her in the course of time.

As far as the substantive elements are concerned, we can say right away that one thing is *absolutely* unchangeable. The Church must necessarily live out her life in the basic liturgical functions of proclamation and sacrament. (This does not mean, however, that the precise shape of each sacramental rite would be definitively fixed.[11]) Outside of these two basic functions, very few substantive elements could be regarded as unchangeable in practice; this is clearly borne out of the history of the liturgy. The historically attested changes have been so profound that we would hardly have the courage to take responsibility for initiating some of them today.[12]

Despite these far-reaching changes, some material and substantive elements of the liturgy are unchangeable, but their immutability must be proven rather than taken for granted at the start. Unlike the unchangeable structures of a more formal nature, they cannot be deduced from the basic postulates of theological anthropology; they derive instead from revelation as it has actually taken place. If the immutability of these liturgical

[11] See K. Rahner, *Kirche und Sakramente* (Freiburg/Breisgau, ²1961); *idem,* "Die Sakramente als Grundfunktionen der Kirche," in *HPTh* I, pp. 323-32.

[12] A striking example is provided by the changes that have taken place in the understanding and the rites of confession during the history of the Church. See B. Potschmann, *Busse und letzte Ölung* (Freiburg/Breisgau, 1951); K. Rahner, "Bussdisziplin, altkirchliche," in *LThK* II, pp. 805-15. The last significant change before the Council dealt with priestly ordination, as Pius XII decreed that only the laying on of hands, together with the ordination prayers, were essential for validity; cf. *Apostolic Constitution Sacramentum Ordinis,* November 30, 1947 (DS 3857).

elements is indeed based on divine precept, this can and must be demonstrated.

If such a demonstration cannot be provided, only the will of God, insofar as it is *ascertainable in history* and sought out there continually, can determine how and what changes may legitimately be introduced. When it is a question of the substantive and material elements, we only know that we *can* celebrate the liturgy as the Church has done in the past. That we *must* do it in this way is something to be proved, as is the assertion that we *should* do it some other way.

V

LEAVING ROOM FOR CHANGE

It is obvious from the foregoing that loyalty to tradition is not the sole reason why the Church maintains the forms of liturgy transmitted to her by Christ through the primitive community. The basic cast of baptism and the eucharist, for example, is not the product of whim; these liturgical forms can be shown to be obligatory, and they must be regarded as immutable.

We can also see why the Church maintains and reverently preserves *her traditions,* especially those going back to the apostolic age. It may indeed be necessary for her to look for new forms when circumstances change. With the salvation of mankind as her objective, she may decide that change is necessary if she is to remain true to her mission, if men are "to imitate Christ more closely".[13] The history of the liturgy and sacramental theology prove conclusively that far-reaching changes have indeed taken place. The traditions themselves have undergone *growth.*

To say this is not to advocate change or innovation for its own sake. But history and theology do show that change is not only possible but sometimes necessary. It is necessary when the old forms conceal rather than reveal the real import of the liturgy.[14]

[13] St. Ignatius, *Exercises,* n. 167.
[14] The necessity for establishing rites, customs and forms for cultic

Whether change is necessary or not at a given moment must be determined on the basis of the concrete historical situation. This means that ecclesiastical authorities must read and heed the "signs of the times", and that they must leave sufficient room for new liturgical forms to take shape in the concrete life of the community.

Today this open room seems to be quite restricted because a sharp polarity has taken shape. One group is seeking to preserve the old and partially frozen liturgy of a bygone age. The other group is pressing to refashion this same liturgy as much as possible, or as much as seems necessary. Thus respect for tradition and the desire for reform are clashing head-on over the same object: the Latin liturgy of the Roman rite. How could tension be avoided when one group thinks there has been too much change and the other group thinks there has been too little? Is it any wonder that the efforts of the reformers have aroused conservative opposition?

A single uniform liturgy for the whole Church—be it old-style or new-style—seems hardly desirable or practicable. Perhaps it would have been better to leave the pre-conciliar liturgy unchanged and, at the same time, allow more room for the development of new liturgical forms that need not be so bound to past traditions. The resultant new forms, standing alongside the old liturgy instead of replacing it, could then give rise to fruitful interaction between both liturgical forms.

On the whole, then, liturgical forms must undergo some change. However we may approach it in a given instance, we must weigh carefully the justification and the extent of such change. We must take into account the history of the liturgy and the insights of sacramental theology. We must also consider—and this is too often overlooked—the viewpoints of the anthropological and social sciences: sociology, psychology, pedagogy, etc. Such considerations must also be given more place in our

---

worship is paralleled by the necessity of constantly reviewing them. We must never cease to ask ourselves whether they still truly and clearly embody the intentions they are meant to embody.

experimental services than they have been up to now, for liturgy is a concrete activity more than a theoretical discipline.

After a suitable testing period, the competent ecclesiastical authorities should and must say yes or no to the changes. The judgment will bind the whole Church or a given segment of the Church, as the case may be. In either case it will be the Church speaking as the *ekklesia*—that is, as the salvation community in which Christ lives on and to which the liturgical worship of Jesus Christ is entrusted during the course of history.[15]

[15] See K. Rahner-L. Hofmann, "Die Disziplin in der Kirche," in *HPTh* I, pp. 33-36. For other questions touched upon in this article, see H. B. Meyer, *Lebendige Liturgie* (Innsbruck, 1966); *idem*, "Von der liturgischen Erneuerung zur Erneuerung der Liturgie," in *StdZ* 175 (1964/65), pp. 81-97; *idem*, "Una Voce: Nunc et Semper?" in *StdZ* 180 (1967), pp. 73-90, or in *Bibel und Liturgie* 40 (1967), pp. 330-48; *idem*, "Die Bibel in Liturgie und Verkündigung," in *Bibel und Liturgie* 40 (1967), pp. 287-304.

Salvatore Marsili, O.S.B./*Rome, Italy*

Liturgical Texts
for Modern Man

In his attempt to give a summary view of the Roman liturgy as a whole, E. Bishop spoke with good reason of a "genius" of the Roman rite [1] and said that its study entails putting forth "an effort that allows the affirmation and recognition of the particular and native spirit by which a rite is so animated and pervaded as to result in a rite differentiated from the others".[2]

I

THE TRANSLATION OF LITURGICAL TEXTS

If this preliminary observation of Bishop had worth as a general introduction to an understanding of the Roman liturgy viewed as an historic and cultural phenomenon in its totality of formularies and ceremonies, it seems to us that we must refer to it even more with respect to the translation of liturgical texts which must pass from the original Latin language to modern languages. In other words, at the basis of every translation we must prefix a study—made up of reflection as well as a certain

[1] Ed. Bishop, *Liturgica historica* (Oxford, 1918), pp. 1-19. A French translation, with adaptations and interesting supplementary notes, was made by A. Wilmart, *Le génie du rit romain* (Paris, 1920).
[2] *Ibid.*, p. 2.

49

psychologico-linguistic sensitivity—which allows us to identify first the "genius" of the Latin language and then the "genius" of the modern language into which it is translated.

Hence, we could not regard as scientific a translation based on the belief that the sense of a Latin text could be captured by simple recourse to a dictionary and study of the grammatical and logical form in question. For the form obeys determined grammatical rules and certain constructions not so much by reason of some external linguistic laws; it does so more out of the impulse of that element which is "intangible and indefinable and nevertheless immanent and capable of being perceived and which forms the particular and distinctive spirit"; [3] this reveals precisely the "genius" of the text under discussion, which is in turn the "genius" of the people, the age, and the culture giving rise to the text.

Naturally, in dealing with translations from a language such as Latin which already has a very rich history in itself, it must be prejudicially admitted that an "original" interpretation of it will be impossible unless account is taken of the various factors which appear in this particular expression which is the Latin-Christian-liturgical language. For this is complicated by other elements—besides the linguistic moments already highly differentiated among one another expressed in the term—which while seeming to be accessory and possibly secondary are nonetheless determinative since they constitute further evolutions in the very "genius" of the language. We refer to the theological elements from definite periods, the literary or thought influences stemming from particular persons and circles, moments of high or low spiritual tension, diverse cultural currents, and phenomena of literary traditionalism accompanied in turn by profound transformations of thought whether on the general theological plane or on the liturgical plane in particular.

All this produces a strange and complicated situation in the texts. For the Latin liturgy is not a monolithic block created at one and the same time or in one and the same place; hence, it is

[3] *Ibid.*

obliged time after time to discover in its formularies the particular characteristics which can blossom therein. Then there will be no delay in realizing that while it retains certain constant lines, the "genius" of the Roman liturgy reveals other elements which are very exactly evaluated and localized in space and time in order to be translated in a suitable fashion.

Everyone knows that the polemics which continually arise concerning translations stem precisely from the question as to whether it is necessary or suitable to lose or retain this "genius" of the ancient language which has become for the most part also the "genius" of the Latin liturgy. To lose it—the assertion is made—would be to disfigure the face of the liturgy because it would be divested of something traditional to it. To retain it—is the reply—would mean to prevent the liturgy from ever becoming a real part of *our* life.

II
THE PRINCIPAL ELEMENTS OF LITURGICAL LATIN

Perhaps it is necessary to introduce distinctions and precisions into the elements of liturgical Latin. Though we are unable to dwell on all the secondary elements mentioned above, we must nevertheless take account at least of the principal ones.

The Latin Element

This is the basic element used not only in evangelization but also in the liturgy, at least from the moment (toward the end of the 3rd century) when Latin began to be spoken (and Greek abandoned) at Rome. Naturally, the Latin style in question in the liturgical texts is not the style known as "classical" but the style current at a certain epoch; simultaneously with structures of a classical character and tendencies stemming from the "new" style mentioned by Mohrmann,[4] this incorporates a style that

[4] Cf. Mohrmann, *Etudes sur le latin des chrétiens* III (Rome, 1965), pp. 153ff.

prefers the paratactical form and readily has recourse to both simple and antithetical parallelism. Here are a few examples in the Latin liturgical formularies:

(1) *Simple parallelism*
"Largire supplicibus tuis ut cogitemus
te inspirante,
quae recta sunt,
et te gubernante,
eadem faciamus" (*5th Sun. after Pent.*).

"Ut nullius sit irritum votum,
nullius vacua postulatio,
praesta ut,
quod fideliter petimus,
efficaciter consequamur" (*Super obl.—6th Sun. after Pent.*).

(2) *Antithetical parallelism*
"Ut quae sunt bona
nutrias
ac pietatis studio
quae sunt nutrita
custodias" (*6th Sun. after Pent.*).

"Ut noxia cuncta
submoveas
et omnia nobis profutura
concedas" (*7th Sun. after Pent.*).

"Quod singuli obtulerunt
ad maiestatis tuae honorem
cunctis proficiat
ad salutem" (*Super obl.—7th Sun. after Pent.*).

"Largire nobis . . . semper spiritum
cogitandi

quae recta sunt
propitius et agendi:
ut qui sine te
esse non possumus
secundum te
vivere valeamus" (*8th Sun. after Pent.*).

(3) *Paratactical style with alternation of synthetical (1) and antithetical (2) parallelism*
"Sit in eis, Domine, per donum Spiritus tui

(1) prudens modestia,
    sapiens benignitas,
    gravis lenitas,
    casta libertas.

(2) In caritate ferveant
    et nihil extra te diligant;
    laudabiliter vivant
    laudarique non appetant.
    Te in sanctitate corporis,
    te in animi sui puritate
    glorificent.

(1)+(2) Amore
    te timeant,
    amore
    tibi serviant.

(1) Tu eis honor
    tu gaudium
    tu voluntas.

(2) Tu in moerore
    solacium,
    tu in ambiguitate
    consilium,
    tu in iniuria
    defensio,
    in tribulatione
    patientia,

in paupertate
abundantia,
in ieiunio
cibus,
in infirmitate
medicina.
In te habeant
omnia
quem elegere
super omnia" (*Pont. Rom., De ben. et cons. vir-
ginum*. Cf. *Sacrament. Veron.*, Mohlberg 1104.
For an analogous form, cf. the nuptial blessing of
the Missal and in the *Sacram. Veron.*, Mohlberg
1110).

Another characteristic of Latin style is the tendency to ac-
cumulate similar expressions resulting in a redundancy of style
which would seem to be contrary to the ever glorified expressive
sobriety of the Roman formularies. The most probative examples
are precisely in the *Roman Canon*, with its binary, ternary,
quaternary and quinary clauses:

bin.:   "supplices rogamus ac petimus"
        "uti accepta habeas et benedicas"
ter.:   "haec dona, haec munera, haec sancta"
quat.:   "quam pacificare, custodire, adunare et regere"
bin.:   "fides . . . devotio"
ter.:   "pro se suisque omnibus
        pro redemptione animarum suarum
        pro spe salutis et incolumitatis suae"
        "aeterno Deo vivo et vero"
quin.:   "benedictam adscriptam ratam rationalilem ac-
        ceptabilemque"
ter.:   "hostiam puram, hostiam sanctam, hostiam im-
        maculatam"

bin.:   "panem sanctum vitae aeternae
          et calicem salutis perpetuae"

The same style is found, for example, in the formularies of the Preface and other consecratory prayers: "Domine, sancte Pater, omnipotens aeterne Deus", which in the prayers for the ordination of deacons is prolonged by: "donorum dator ordinumque distributor atque officiorum dispositor" (*Pont. Rom;* cf. *In ord. presbyt.* therein). We must also assign to this style—though constituted in a relative position—a few amply descriptive formularies like the one that recurs in the *Blessing of the baptismal font:*

"Deus cuius spiritus super aquas. . . .
 Deus qui nocentis mundi crimina. . . .
 Per Deum qui te in principio. . . .
     qui te de paradisi fonte. . . .
     qui te in deserto amaram. . . .
 Per Iesum Christum . . . qui te in Cana Galileae . . .
     qui pedibus super te ambulavit. . . .
     qui te una cum sanguine de latere suo produxit"
 (*Rom. Missal;* cf. *Sacr. Gelas.,* Mohlberg 445-446).

This verbal redundancy must be accurately gauged. That is, we must not accord an excessive significance to this accumulation of attributes and epithets; although they possess a deliberate theological intent, they stem principally from stylistic exigencies. At the same time they must not be interpreted as useless "verbosity"; they are witnesses of a certain *cultural* style, transmitted to the liturgy from usage and from the pre-Christian Roman religious mentality, as can be seen by the ancient formulas of Roman prayers that are preserved for us; [5] the accumulation of titles and the most detailed requests in such prayers denotes the

[5] Three of these ancient formularies are found in Mohrmann, *loc. cit.,* pp. 237ff. Cf. other examples in Brissonius, *De formulis et sollemnibus, libri VIII* (Frankfurt, 1592), pp. 55, 57, 71.

concern that the prayer be the most complete possible, and express and signify everything, without leaving anything uncertain.

This is the sense of Roman *juridic precision* which is revealed in worship and passes—at the basis of a connatural *mentality*—also into Christian formularies. And proof that we are concerned with a *stylistico-religious tradition* is found in the fact that this style appears chiefly in solemn formularies; the Canon must be regarded as such, even though it is in daily use.

Hence, faced as we are with stylistic facts that are clearly identifiable, what should be our reaction in the translation? We obviously do not wish to deny that this *Latin style* has for centuries characterized the liturgical formularies to the point of creating that typical *mentality* recognized as proper to liturgical prayer which has come down to us as its characteristic. The problem posed is whether we must preserve the *mentality* received by this tradition and separate it from its *style*. There is indeed agreement that a *non-Latin liturgy* should have a non-Latin style of its own.

However, even in relation to the above-mentioned "mentality" it seems to us that it is not so much the mentality that *expressed* itself in the style as it is the style that *formed* it by obeying certain interim constructive laws and exigencies which came to the style from the very "genius" of the people and the cultural age in which it acted. Thus the very necessity which arises to abandon the style justifies diminishing the mentality which concurs with it in the same "genius" that was valid formerly but no longer today. A translation which would fail to carry out this twofold separation would create solely a pseudo-modern text, because it would still be conditioned by the stylistico-mental element of the Latin.

We believe an example of how this might come to pass can be found—at least to a notable extent—in the most challenging translation of those produced till the present time, notwithstanding the limitations imposed by authority. We are speaking of the *Roman Canon,* and we believe we can single out in this respect the *English translation;* through the use of direct sentences, with an absolutely essential language, brief and stripped of all redundancy, it has given the formula "Te igitur" of the Canon a flavor that is modern and certainly "congenial" to the English taste.[6]

This incurs the objection that it brings about the loss of "traditional" elements of the liturgy to the extent of having it assume an appearance that is very different from the Latin liturgy from which it stems; the reply is that a certain *stylistic form,* with annexed *thought-values,* does not form part of the "tradition" which concerns the liturgy. It is an easy and understandable error, but an error nonetheless, to transform a "stylistic" fact into a fact of "tradition" on the liturgical plane. For the former is a *static* value, a cultural note of a definite people and epoch; the latter is instead living *transmission* of a religious thought which can never be reasonably identified with the basic structure. Hence, even admitting that a "style" can invest the "tradition" to the extent of giving it a particular tone and emphases which cannot be distinguished from one another because the former is transitory and the latter perennial, we must strip the "tradition" of its stylistic "covering" precisely so that it can still be living and true "tradition"—that is, valid also for our times which have a different style.

In conclusion: in order for "tradition" to be "translated" effectively into a modern language it must be stripped of its *Latin element* and all the implications with which it is invested.

---

[6] However, by this statement we do not wish to endorse the translation of *"una cum* papa. . . ."* by the words: "We offer them *for* N., our pope." In addition to the alteration of a traditional theological value (the eucharist is either celebrated by the bishop or is celebrated *in union with* the bishop: unity of the Church around the vicar of Christ, the bishop), there has also been an evident lack in the reading of the Latin text and in the understanding of its style. The relative clause "Quam pacificare . . . terrarum" is so dependent or subordinate as to constitute almost a parenthesis, possessing the value of an appositive clause, which should not impede—even if it made it more difficult—the natural union of the verb "offerimus pro . . . una cum papa" (we offer you for . . . together with the pope). In reality the English translation saw the connection between "offerimus" and "una cum", so much so that it repeated the verb "we offer", but it did not grasp the theological meaning, and so translated "una cum" by "for", doing violence to the dictionary.

The Christian-Liturgical Element

It is a fact known to all historians of the Latin language that at a definite time this language was not only fermented with a new content of thought—the Christian content—but also enriched with a new vocabulary and new forms of expression. "The current language was thus subjected to an evolution in which Christian thought was determinative to the point of forging a real particular language, the language of a group of Christians." [7] The starting point of this new linguistic fermentation which gives new physiognomy to the ancient Latin is placed in the Christian religious fact which, erupting in the Latin world, acts through two divergent and convergent paths on the formation of the *Christian-liturgical Latin* language.

On the one hand, there is *preaching* which deliberately keeps its distance from the literary form, makes more ready use of the "popular" tongue, and has as its content truth and realities which above all easily preserve their adherence to the proper original form of expression already found in the Hebrew religion that serves as its basis. In other words, in transmitting the new Christian content, preaching tends, as is natural, to transmit it in the form most connatural to it—because it stems from the original—and thus becomes a new and entirely innovative element of the language into which it is transferred.

The other path utilized by Christianity to penetrate deeply into the Latin linguistic world proceeds through the *translation of the Bible*. In making such a translation the first Christians "did not follow the lines of translation already established among others by Cicero, but were inspired rather by the Jewish method. Although classical antiquity both in theory and practice was in favor of free translation which entailed a certain amount of reworking and adaptation of the text in accord with the genius of the particular language, in translating the Bible Christians followed their Hebrew ancestors who confined themselves to a kind of literalism out of respect for the text and translated word for

[7] Mohrmann, *loc. cit.*, p. 147.

word. The result was literal translations which, in addition to being made from Greek texts already encumbered with a certain exoticism, remained completely outside the traditional rules applicable for the creation of a literary work, having as their sole concern to reproduce the original text scrupulously and with slavish fidelity, with the consequence of creating vocabulary and semantic neologisms, making numerous castings, and finally syntactical innovations".[8]

Given the profound influence exerted by biblical language over Christian Latin, the latter appears from then on as a content which, except for its Semitic colorings, is enclosed within precise categories. One is obviously the *biblico-revealed category,* and the other is given by the *ideological dimension* of the epoch; and it is the latter which confers its conceptual and expressive coating onto revealed values in order to introduce them into the surrounding world.

Biblico-revealed categories are, for example: salvation—redemption; Easter—saving sacrifice of Christ; People of God—Church—kingdom of God; appearance or manifestation of Christ—day of the Lord; death—resurrection—life—light; love of God—glory of God—will of the Father—plan of salvation—sanctification; the Lord's supper—baptism—remission of sins, etc.

As ideological categories we have in mind—for the time of the primitive Church—a whole complex of ideas partly revealed and partly deduced from the revelation which was acclimatized into already existing modes of thought. We think of: sacrament—mystery; order—clergy; regeneration—communion—peace, etc.

It is clear that the first of these categories are too closely connected with revelation for us to think of excluding them from our translations. To do so would mean to destroy nothing less than the human linguistic "symbols" and "signs" used by revelation in presenting itself to the world precisely as a "word". Concerning the rest of the categories, we must say in analogous fashion: although they have in some way respectively "Hellenized" or

[8] *Ibid.,* p. 148.

"Latinized" the Christian reality and given it a casing that is in itself conditioned by a definite time and culture, they have also entered in too profound a "symbiosis" with Christianity for this to be undone for certain.

We do not thereby wish to deny that a certain "de-Latinizing" of the liturgical texts can be useful and above all possible. In the theological field we have seen the occurrence in Scholasticism of a certain process of "de-Hellenization", and a similar process— though in greater forms—seems to be announcing itself with the "new" theology. But even apart from the fact that there is no unanimity as yet in establishing the limits of such a process and even less concerning its real utility, the possibilities of the liturgy in this field could be different from those of theology, in the same way that the possibilities of life (liturgy) are different from those of science (theology).

III
NEW LITURGICAL LANGUAGE

However, we believe that what perhaps cannot be obtained by remaining along the lines of "translation" can be achieved along the lines of the "creation" of a *new liturgical language*.

While remaining within the lines of traditional structures, the liturgical renewal of Vatican Council II not only goes beyond the value of a rubrical fact but in the very preservation of these structures also tends toward "something *new,* and indeed toward something living for living men".[9] For the Council speaks of a renewal that reduces the rites to a noble simplicity, effected through clarity and brevity (*Sacr. Conc.,* 34), "so that they express more clearly the holy things which they signify; the Christian people, as far as possible, should be enabled to understand them with ease and to take part in them fully, actively and as befits a community" (*ibid.,* 21). This must be achieved by the

[9] Cf. *Notitiae* (1965), p. 254.

translations of the texts into different languages (*ibid.*, 36, 54, 63, 101, 113) but also by an effort of *adaptation* which can be a very radical one, in order to be equal to the genius and cultural traditions of individual peoples (*ibid.*, 40).

All of this means much more than the application of a few revisions—even radical ones—to the current liturgy. Indeed, the renewal of Vatican Council II is a *door opened on the future* more than an attempt to safeguard an inheritance of the past. That is to say, once provision has been made for the retention of "sane tradition" which is certainly not that translation frozen in formulas, the Council intends "that the way remain open to legitimate progress" (*ibid.*, 23). As for the consequences and terminus of this longed-for "legitimate progress", they are explicitly set forth in the same article cited (n. 23). They are really and truly "innovations"—that is, "new forms"—which the liturgy could assume. Indeed, even if in this respect it is stated that in principle "there must be no innovations", their exclusive is conditioned only by the stipulation "unless the good of the Church generally and certainly requires this". However, if this point is verified and if the "innovations" should "grow organically from forms already existing", then their presence is included in the "legitimate progress" desired for the liturgy.

Therefore with the prior necessary accord of the ecclesiastical authority, whether peripheral or central, according to competence but also with the prejudgment that the same authority neither wishes to nor should ignore this conciliar "breakthrough" except for grave reasons, there is the *possibility*—and, considering the real situation, we should say: there is the *necessity*—of creating "new liturgical forms". Speaking only of the Mass, this means: preserving the basic element of the *faith* according to which the Mass is both the sacrifice of Christ and of the Church and the paschal banquet; and taking into account the fact that through *tradition* it must be the proclamation of the mystery of Christ in the Word and in the communitary celebration by means of a "prayer of thanksgiving", which has as object the "history of salvation", it is admitted that all these elements can assume "new forms" as long as they constitute "progress and organic growth over the preceding ones".

Could we say that the *translations* are the longed-for "new forms" and that they respond to the "legitimate progress" to which the Council "opens the way"? We might say that Pope Paul himself timidly placed the point in doubt when he said: "Now the versions are parts of the rites themselves; they are the voice of the Church. The *spoken tongue* which now takes its place in the liturgy must be adapted to the understanding of all." [10]

For we can ask with profound and justified uneasiness whether the translations truly create the climate of understanding demanded by the liturgy, not only because of the difficulties inherent in them as a result of the reasons given above, but also because it can be asked whether the liturgical thought itself has always received the best expression in them or, above all, the one adapted to every time. It is sufficient to reflect on the inertia of spiritual movement with which the first oration for Easter Sunday is concluded—after having spoken of a "gate of everlasting life" opened to us through the resurrection of Christ—in order to answer the question in the negative.[11]

But there is no reason to tarry over other examples, since the translations themselves—necessary and useful though they are —nowadays ever more reveal their insufficiency. Although these formularies originated in a profoundly Christian climate, they did so as part of visions which were different from our daily situations, and they come across in translation for us as if— beautiful and bloodless—they were reaching us from a world too distant from our own. If the liturgy had always been a living fact,

---

[10] Discourse to the translators of liturgical books (Nov. 10, 1965) in *Le traduzioni dei libri liturgici, Atti del congresso* (Rome, 1965), p. 12.

[11] Cf. the authentic conclusion in *Sacr. Gelas.* (Mohlberg, 463), which referring ("per innovationem tui spiritus") to the vision of Ez. 37, 1-14, recalled the fulfillment of the divine promise: "You shall know that I am the Lord, when I open your graves. . . . I will put my spirit in you that you may live. . . ."

perhaps today its formularies would still be close to us. But the fact is that too many Christian generations have been on the margin of the liturgy; and if our generation is suddenly thrust before the liturgy today, it is almost impossible for this generation to enter effectively into the liturgical mystery if this is still couched in an arcane language, notwithstanding the faithfulness of the translation.

If a *new* liturgical language is not created, the liturgy will remain always and uniquely a "festive garment" which, as we know, can have even exotic forms and colors that glitter but fail to express what lies within them. Above all, this would be the sign that our theology has not rethought revelation as something new, as the announcement of presence (kerygma), and that the "eternal" reality of the "history of salvation" has not been "temporalized" in a language which "incarnates" it in our time, and that therefore it has ceased to be a "history" and remained only the "account" of a history made in terms and accents of other times.

But today, precisely because of the summons of Vatican Council II, there is ever increasing lively awareness that not only did God speak "in divers manners . . . in times past (*olim*)" but also "at the end of these days (*novissime*)—[that is, today, he] has spoken to us by his Son" (Heb. 1, 1-2); therefore, it is just and proper that we respond to this modern Word with a *new liturgy* that is equally modern and not merely with translations. Only in this way will the liturgy cease to be a "monument of the past" and become an expression of the mystery of Christ and of the Church in the "present moment".

By doing this the Church will take up again the method and spirit which were recognized as valid in the early centuries (1st to 8th centuries), and which in restricted measure were applied even in the Middle Ages. In fact, we must recognize the fact that before the issuance of the Bull *Immensa* of Sixtus V (January 22, 1588), establishing the Congregation of Rites *"to preserve . . . and cause to be preserved the ancient rites everywhere* and by everyone", the first attempt toward liturgical immutability came not from the Church but from the civil power (Pepin and Charlemagne), followed afterward by analogous indications with Gregory VII (11th century) and Innocent III (13th century).

However, nowadays the Church herself—even though she is still officially tied down to the ancient formularies in the very creation of new formularies (cf. the recent *Preces eucharisticae*)—clearly demonstrates that she regards attempts at more profound renewal as neither impossible nor inadmissible. Already, in the case of the *Third World Congress for the Apostolate of the Laity* (Rome, 1967) not only was permission officially granted to choose *readings* and *biblical chants* adapted to the subject of study on the individual days, but the concession was also given for composing absolutely original *entrance chants* for each day's Mass. Here are a few extracts:

1. Peuples, criez de joie et bondissez d'allégresse,
   Le Père envoie le Fils manifester sa tendresse:
   Ouvrons les yeux: Il est l'Image de Dieu
   Pour que chacun le connaisse.
2. Loué soit notre Dieu, maître et Seigneur de ce monde:
   Ses mains ont tout créé pour que nos coeurs lui répondent:
   Par Jésus-Christ, Il donne l'être et la vie
   Pour que sa Vie surabonde. . . .3. . . .4. . . .5. . . .

1. Peuple de Dieu, n'aie pas de honte,
   Montre ton signe à ce temps-ci!
   En traversant l'âge du monde,
   Cherche ton souffle dans l'Esprit;
   Tourne à sa grâce ton penchant:
   Pour qu'il habite tes louanges
   et soit visible en ses enfants. . . .2. . . .3. . . .4. . . .

1. Vous êtes sans pareille,
   O mere du Sauveur! (*bis*)
   Vous êtes la merveille

Des oeuvres du Seigneur,
  O Notre Dame,
Des oeuvres du Seigneur . . . . 2 . . . . 3 . . . . 4 . . . . [11a]

But even in the sphere of the *orations* of the Mass, newness
has been officially accepted on occasion of an *Ecumenical Meeting of the Leaders of Intra-European Migrations* (Bossey, Switzerland, May, 1968). The orations are formulated as follows:

ORAZIONE. Preghiamo. . . : O Dio/tu hai voluto che tuo
Figlio si facesse/viandante fra gli uomini/per tutti riunire
in una sola famiglia da condurre a te;/guarda a tutti coloro
che nella dispersione si sforzano di vivere nella fedeltà a
te,/perche il tuo nome sia onorato fra le genti/e ogni loro
azione diventi un segno del tuo amore. Per. . . .

ORAZIONE SOPRA LE OFFERTE. L'offerta comune di
questi doni/esprime a te, Signore, il nostro impegno e i

[11a] 1. All you peoples, shout with joy and leap for gladness,
    The Father sends the Son to manifest his compassion:
    Let us open our eyes: He is the Image of God
    So that each one may know him.
  2. Praised be our God, Lord and Master of the world:
    His hands have created everything so that our hearts might respond to him:
    Through Jesus Christ he gives existence and life
    So that his Life may superabound . . . . 3 . . . . 4 . . . . 5 . . . .

  1. People of God, do not be ashamed,
    Show your sign to this age!
    In traversing the age of this world,
    Seek your inspiration in the Spirit;
    Let your inclinations be influenced by his grace:
    So that he may invest your praises
    and be visible in his children . . . . 2 . . . . 3 . . . . 4 . . . .

  1. You are without equal
    O mother of the Savior! (*bis*)
    You are the marvel
    Of the works of the Lord,
      O our Lady,
    Of the works of the Lord . . . . 2 . . . . 3 . . . . 4 . . . .

nostri desideri di unità;/per l'azione dello Spirito S. diventi essa sacrificio che ci purifichi dalle colpe e ci vincoli nella carità. Per. . . .

ORAZIONE DOPO LA COMUNIONE. La partecipatione a/questo convito, Signore, ci ha gioiosamente uniti a te;/ fa che nella carità operosa a servizio degli uomini/sappiamo superare ogni divisione e giungere a spezzare insieme il pane di vita. Per. . . .[12]

As can be seen, the orations are profoundly pointed to the particular assembly and practically conditioned by it and by its needs and intentions. The last two formularies with their call for *unity* and with the hope that we can one day "succeed in *breaking* the bread of life *in common*" make a clear and completely delicate reference to those separated brethren who though present at the eucharistic celebration were nevertheless unable to participate with the others in the Lord's table.

A few formularies of new liturgical prayers are known to us by a study of H. Schmidt who establishes a comparison for each of them between the translation of the *ancient* formulary and the *new* formulary:

3rd SUNDAY OF ADVENT (After Communion)

Trans.: Nous implorons, Seigneur, ta douceur et ta bonté, afin

---

[12] The Italian text is taken from a cyclostile copy distributed on the day of the *Meeting*. PRAYER. Let us pray. . . : O God,/you willed that your Son should become a wayfarer among men/in order to unite all men into a single body and lead them to you;/look upon all those who in their separation strive to live in fidelity to you,/so that your name may be honored among the peoples/and their every act may become a sign of your love. Through. . . . PRAYER OVER THE GIFTS. May the common offering of these gifts/express to you, O Lord, our pledge and desires of unity;/through the action of the Holy Spirit may this become a sacrifice that purifies us from our faults and binds us together in love. Through . . . . PRAYER AFTER COMMUNION. Our participation in this banquet, O Lord, has joyously united us to you;/grant that through active love in the service of men/we may be able to surpass every division and succeed in *breaking* the bread of life *together*. Through . . . .

que, soutenus par cette communion et guéris de nos penchants mauvais, nous nous préparions aux fêtes qui approchent.

New: Seigneur Dieu, Père toutpuissant, tu as envoyé ton fils parminous comme un inconnu; c'est ainsi qu'il est au milieu de nous, s'étant fait le moindre des hommes. Nous te prions afin que nous puissions le reconnaître dans tous ceux qui nous entourent, surtout dans ceux qui sont faibles et sans prestige.

16th SUNDAY AFTER PENETCOST

New: Seigneur Dieu, tu nous a donné la première place dans ta création tandis que toi-même tu t'es fait le dernier, invisible comme le souffle du vent, imperceptible comme le silence. . . .[13]

We have reproduced two of the five formularies referred to by Schmidt which we believe to be indicative as to how a liturgical prayer can be at the same time profoundly inserted in the present spiritual context, in the form of a grand human dignity, and can get closer (1st formulary) to the liturgical mystery (Advent) with clear reference to the idea of the gospel of the day. Perhaps the reference is placed too exclusively on the "human" dimension of the presence of Christ which disappears somewhat as directly redemptive presence.

In other formularies not cited by us, which also concern Advent, the liturgical season seemingly has no influence whatever. This is an inconvenience which could be serious, since we must

[13] H. Schmidt, "Le renouveau liturgique," in *Nouvelle Revue Theol.* 98 (1966), p. 820. The author cautions that these prayers have been taken from H. Manders, "Desacralisering van de Liturgie," in *Theologie en Zielzorg* 62 (1966), 129-43. 3rd SUNDAY OF ADVENT (After Communion): *Trans.:* O Lord, we beg your kindness and goodness, so that, strengthened by this communion and healed of our evil inclinations, we may prepare for the approaching feasts. *New:* Lord God, Father almighty, you have sent your Son among us as an unknown; and he is in the midst of us in this way, having become the least of men. We beg you that we may be able to recognize him in all those around us, especially in those who are weak and without prestige. 16th SUNDAY AFTER PENTECOST: *New:* O Lord God, you have given us first place in your creation while you yourself have become the last, invisible as a puff of wind, imperceptible as silence. . . .

not forget that the liturgical formulary is of *generically religious* prayer, intended solely to express the relation between God and man in some way. It must express this relation "in Christ"—that is, always within the framework of the "history of salvation", of which the liturgy is at once both actuation and "sign".

From this point of view, the formularies given by H. Oosterhuis [14] seem to be good examples. The author cautions that the majority of these prayers "have been used *in experimental fashion* in the liturgical center "Werkgroep voor Volkstaalliturgie" of Amsterdam, which leads us to believe that even here permission has been granted by the competent authority. In this case also we wish to give only a few examples which seem interesting to us, according to the seasons to which the formularies are assigned by an index in this volume.

ADVENT: + You wait for us
until we are open to you.
We wait for your word
to make us receptive.
Attune us to your voice,
to your silence,
speak and bring your son to us—
Jesus, the word of your peace.

CHRISTMAS: + Lord God and father of Jesus Christ
this is the night when he was born,
our hope and our salvation.
We pray to you
to let his light shine in our lives,
may we love him and keep him,
your word among us,
your peace on earth,
today and every day,
world without end.

[14] H. Oosterhuis, *Quelqu'un parmi nous* (Paris, 1968), p. 161; Eng. ed.: *Your Word Is Near* (New York, 1968).

EASTER: + We worship and admire you, God,
               because you have shown your power
               in Jesus Christ,
               raising him from the dead
               and setting him at your right hand,
               exalting him above all powers
               and giving him a name
               which is above every name in this world.
               We ask you
               that we who believe in him
               may be of his mind as well,
               that we may be a sign
               of his life,
               light and peace to all
               who seek you, today
               and every day of our lives.

What is most pleasing about these orations and about so many others not reproduced here is their form which is entirely immersed in the living existence of today, the contact with the liturgical mystery, the profoundly biblical inspiration—even if discrete and quasi-hidden—and that magnificent centrality of Christ which almost always constitutes the explicit center of the oration, which is still always directed to the Father in accord with ancient liturgical tradition. (But why is he always called solely by the name of "God"?)

Finally, we wish to cite precisely the "eucharistic prayer",[15] in which the expert will clearly rediscover the movement of the Hebrew "berakkà-eucaristia", but everyone will be able to find a well-balanced development of the "history of salvation" which tends as to its vertex toward the sacrament-sacrifice of the body and blood of the Lord. Through the liturgical action this continues and makes the Pentecostal coming of the Spirit the element by means of which the Church—having become the "com-

---

[15] *Ibid.*, pp. 117-20.

munity of the Holy Spirit"—can glorify God in Christ, through Christ, and with Christ.

We have only one criticism: There is not even a remote reference to the "paschal banquet" so that the eucharistic prayer seems to remain unto itself as an act of praise of God and not as a concrete actuation of the "history of salvation"—for which thanksgiving was specifically being offered.

The journey toward a *new and living liturgy* is still a long one, but it has begun. And for those who believe in the power of the Spirit and in the life of the Church this already represents a great deal; for it is the sign that "the way is [being opened] to legitimate progress" which was both promised and permitted by Vatican Council II.

Gino Stefani/*Turin, Italy*

Does the Liturgy Still Need Music?

T he difficulties—at times radical—encountered by the liturgical renewal in implementing its programs concerning music and song, the ever more real threat of a ritual neo-formalism, the excesses of zeal on the part of a "liturgy of enthusiasm", and on the other hand the emergence and spontaneous and arrogant growth of vocal and musical manifestations outside official regulations ultimately call for a discussion of basic questions.

The presence of music and song in worship was formerly taken for granted, and we were limited to interpreting its qualities or, after the Council, its functions. Nowadays, we ask whether this presence is necessary because of theological reasons, or whether it responds to basic anthropological exigencies, or whether it is an activity of Christian culture, or a traditional usage, a Church folklore which is being renewed according to modern styles. The way is thus opened for resolving the problem in question: With what perspectives and in what ways, and under what conditions can we today reasonably accept or encourage vocal and musical activity in celebrations and assemblies of the Christian community?

I
BASES AND INTERPRETATIONS

With respect to music and song in the liturgy, theology seemingly has only interpretations to offer rather than bases. In the past the institution of Christian song was readily traced back to the singing of the *hallel* on the part of Jesus at the Last Supper; today, such a thesis is untenable. As for the exhortations of Paul regarding "psalms and hymns and spiritual songs" (Eph. 5, 19; Col. 3, 16), these were invitations to prayer, divine worship and parenesis which, as far as song is concerned, have no more value than a fervorino of a modern pope on the occasion of a congress of cantors.

Ancient liturgy originates in an oral culture in which vocal expression is strongly articulated and significant. The Christian community invents neither the styles nor the functions of vocal expression, but takes them from a living culture.[1] Do people sing at a feast? Then they will also sing in the liturgy which is a feast. Do people use acclamations in moments of collective enthusiasm? The Christian celebration also has such moments, and hence acclamations of its own.

From corteges, Christian worship takes the practice of processional singing; from shepherds, farmers and seamen, the use of the *jubilus;* from the pagan religions, hymns; and from classical oratory, the gestures of proclamation. As for the psalms, the

[1] This position, already adopted by the comparative studies of Doelger, Peterson, Klauser and others, appears ever clearer. Cf., for example, "Iubilus: origini e natura" and "La recitazione delle letture nella liturgia romana antica" in my book *L'acclamation de tout un peuple* (Paris, 1967); Italian ed.: *L'espressione vocale e musicale nella liturgia* (Torino-Leumann, 1967); Spanish ed.: *La aclamación de todo un pueblo* (Madrid, 1967). Cf. also "Exkurs: Iubilare und iubilatio bei Ambrosius" in the work by H. Leeb, *Die Psalmodie bei Ambrosius* (Wien, 1967). A bird's-eye view may be found in my study *L'espressione vocale nella liturgia primitiva* (Rome: Pontifical Liturgical Institute of St. Anselm, 1967, *ad usum manuscriptum*).

typically Christian songs, their importance derives from the text. The psalter is a prayer book, and since its literary form involves lyric poetry, the prayers will often be sung prayers.

The basis for song in the primitive liturgy is therefore entirely anthropological and sociological. The same is not true of the word, which finds its justification in the structure of revelation. In contradistinction to very many cultural and religious traditions, the Bible does not contain cosmogonic myths in which music is a factor. Even in creation, the word is dominant.

In fact, Hebrew culture, as well as later Christian culture, must defend itself from the temptations of music. It must do so by differentiating itself from pagan worship wherein music is addressed to the gods as an absolute value, as an *opus operatum*, a sacrifice and an act of praise which can substitute for the true piety of the one praying and offering. It must differentiate itself from magical cultures, in which music is an instrument of enchantment and bind the human will by superior or inferior powers. It must differentiate itself from carelessness, from the orgiastic techniques of ecstacy and, closer to our day, from romantic musical celebrations, aesthetic exercises of man's identification with the absolute.

The Fathers of the Church found themselves faced with current usages, recognized their basis and gave them a correct interpretation. In oral cultures, singing is a universal action and hence a spontaneous and pleasing one; as a result, there is singing also in church; for the first few centuries it was never necessary to stimulate the people to sing. And since everything that takes place in the liturgy has a mystagogical value, an entire symbolism of song develops which finds its classical synthesis in Augustine: "Voce cantamus, ut nos excitemus; corde cantamus, ut illi (= Deo) placeamus." [2] The anthropological starting point of such a conception is obvious: "Ut per oblectamenta aurium,

---

[2] *Enarr. in Ps.* 147, 5. On the symbolism of song in the Fathers in general, cf. F. X. Basurco, *El canto cristiano en la tradición primitiva* (Madrid, 1966).

infirmior animus in affectum pietatis assurgat." [3] Indeed, man is also the terminal point for song.

Later, when Christian song will have crystallized in Gregorian chant, monastic musicography will surround this repertory with a mythical aura. Divine origins will be invented for it (the myth of Jubal, the "vision" of Pope Gregory, etc.) and it will be looked upon as immutable and sacred. It will rise before the throne of God with a value of *incensum laudis* which derives to it because of its intrinsic sacrality.[4] Here we are very close to the primitive religions and magical cults. This conception will therefore be applied—with the proper modifications—to other repertories and will receive further development.

In conjunction with romantic aesthetics this will give birth to the idea of sacred music as representation or evocation of the divine. Even today there is talk in some ecclesiastical quarters of the "mystique of the organ" and similar heresies in miniature. Paradoxically, this divinized music comes to be considered on the other hand as a cultural object or vestment. The rubrics take it as an indication of the "solemnity" of a rite: more music, more solemnity; less music, less solemnity. With a tautology that is entirely curial, music is mentioned as necessary in solemn Mass, but it is also stipulated that Mass is solemn substantially because it has music.

Popes will go so far as to promulgate documents on music almost as solemn as those on social teaching or the mystical body. An entire legislation will be elaborated, a *jus musicae liturgicae*.[5] In such a conception music and song lose their human nature—relative and unstable—of a sign and become objects, glittering ornaments of an external worship, or goods

[3] St. Augustine, *Confessions*, X, 33. Cf. my study "L'etica musicale di S. Agostino," in *Jucunda Laudatio* (Venice, 1968), pp. 1-65.

[4] Cf. *"Instituta Patrum de modo psallendi sive cantandi,"* in M. Gerbert, *Scriptores ecclesiastici de musica sacra potissimum* (St. Blasius, 1784), I, 8A; Aureliano Reom., *ibid.*, 59B-60A, 275A; Guido D'A., *ibid.*, II, 50; Aribone, *ibid.*, II, 210B; G. Cottonio, *ibid.*, II, 252B, 260B; Tonale Bernardi, *ibid.*, II, 277B; Elia Salomone, *ibid.*, III, 63B; etc.

[5] Cf. F. Romita, *Ius musicae liturgiae* (Rome, 1947).

("thesaurus") to be jealously preserved and exhibited on great occasions.

This objectual conception still subsists in the conciliar and post-conciliar structure and various formulations. But we must free ourselves completely and definitely from it. Man as he is and the concrete community must once more become both the point of departure and the terminus of expressive activity such as music and song.

II
TOWARD A LITURGY-AS-FEAST

If Augustine were alive today, he would no longer base a complete mystagogical liturgy on song. For ours is no longer an oral culture, and singing is no longer, as a rule, a universally spontaneous and pleasing act. Moreover, the present liturgy has retained its native oral characteristics; it requires specific vocal actions for proclamation and acclamation, for prayer and for hymns, actions which our culture can offer only with difficulty.[6] This accounts for the great difficulty in performing such a liturgy in a satisfactory manner and the diverse evaluation with respect to the past concerning the use of music and song.

A function which is commonly regarded as fundamental for music and song is the feast and the solemnity, terms usually coupled as synonymous. In reality, this synonymity—hence that function—is highly disputable. A feast means freedom, joy, spontaneity, enthusiasm, expressive euphoria, communication and creation. A solemnity on the other hand conjures up gravity, a fixed ceremonial, an archaic flavor, an air of formalism and minutiae. At a feast we are at ease, but a solemnity encourages inhibition. Solemnity of rite goes well with art, whereas the spontaneous act of singing requires an atmosphere of a feast. Indeed,

[6] However, see the writer's proposals in *L'acclamation de tout un peuple, op. cit.*

art is the crystallization of act, as solemnity is the crystallization of feast; and connected with this is the fact that in mass civilizations "art" is often a cultural pursuit.

Typical of our present liturgy is the conflict between demands for expression and inhibiting conditions. Singing is desired but every impediment to the "state of singing" is placed in the way. Modern man is acquainted with feasts, but he does not recognize the liturgy as a feast. The tone of this liturgy is one of solemnity. By pretending to be a feast it only appears ludicrous. How can we offer the Augustinian adage "cantare amantis est" to the faithful who are substantially present only to satisfy a juridico-moral obligation, the Sunday precept? And what significance can a "communion song" have for persons who do not receive the eucharist and do not want to have anything in common with their neighbor?

It would also be easy to show the inhibiting character of the style of the texts, vestments and rites of a good part of the present liturgy, tied as they are to archaic repertories. And when the requirements of the liturgy with regard to singing find a really satisfactory response, the liturgy becomes unhinged. For example, those who attend a "youth Mass" as a rule carry away this impression: the young people function very well and so does their music; it is everything else that does not fit in. If man and his expression are taken seriously, we have a new wine which no longer stays in old wineskins.

Yet the ideal direction of the liturgy should and could coincide with the tendency of contemporary civilization toward the restoration of feasts. The tendency is toward emancipation from servile work and a free activity in which man constructs himself, toward the reacquisition of the numinous, of the natural, of the personal action which frees us from the mechanical, from something reproduced, from what is always equal; the tendency is to surpass materialism and go toward a reading of open and multiple things, toward personal expression and total and universal communication beyond the differences of language and codes, toward communion and community. The Christian celebration of the future must be able to fit without irony and misconception into the program of our weekend. Does not the expressive activity of today constitute a stimulus to all this? By encouraging a reasonable custom of singing and a varied use of music, we are preparing the exigencies of a prayer-reunion in which the rite will be a re-creation.

But the principle for such a preparation is: less solemnity, more feast. Only in a climate of festivity will music and song retain their constant anthropological values and develop favorable conditions for Christian assemblies: spiritual availability which derives from enthusiasm; joy which has diverse paschal suggestions; the renewal of the inner man in this climate of re-creation; eschatological orientation of this humanly ideal situation; communion which is prepared for by expressive communication; etc.

But all this cannot be predetermined by rules and rubrics. The "state of singing" cannot be imposed from without. The truth of the sign requires the actual presence of the signifier and the signified as well as the accurate perception and action of the interpreters. But the pluralism of our society poses so many and such conditions relative to the levels and kinds of faith, modes of perception, styles and repertories, local and personal contexts, as to render vain the expectations based on generally anthropological and religious presuppositions.

A few examples will help to give an awareness of the fullness and profundity of this pluralism in the experience of music and song in contemporary assemblies.

III
RESONANT EVENTS AND MESSAGES

To remain within concrete and realistic dimensions, before speaking of ritual sign and liturgical art we must speak of resonant events and messages. In Christian gatherings resonant events are not always intentionally or consciously expressive; yet they are always significant and they modify the attitude of the faithful. In fact, the experience of the mass media has shown that the suggestion of messages is much more effective when it is less noticeable. Hence, even the less voluntary aspects of a resonant event merit attention.

Material and banal factors often lead to the ruin of an entire mystagogical edifice. For example, an overly loud microphone exaggerates the image of power created by this means of transmission, destroying our efforts at effecting a balance between parallel and lateral relations. Certain echo effects in the arches of a church can create the very aura of mystery which our words wish to de-mythologize. The rhythms of the recitation and the types of vocal emission are sometimes restrained and at other times weak.

IV
WORDS

The preoccupation with music and song begins with the lessening of interest in words. Caesar of Arles laments the fact that the people were participating less and less in singing, but the fact is that his faithful were reaching the point where they no longer understood Latin, and it did not come easy for them to respond by acclaiming a word which they had not understood very well, in a language that dampened enthusiasm. Later on, the musical coating rendered plausible, and even acceptable, speeches that were given in an unknown language and enshrined in venerable sacrality rites that were incomprehensible.

A greater concern for words would reduce the present problematic concerning music. Moreover, such a concern is completely encouraged by the auditors. Words are taken much more seriously than music; their normal reception, even in the mass media, is neither indirect nor distracted. As for the liturgy, in the case of present Christian assemblies, which are only very slightly eucharistic, it is substantially a liturgy of the word and prayer.

V
WHO SINGS IN GROUPS TODAY?

Singing makes the community.[7] But who sings in groups today? The diffusion of the means of sound reproduction has dealt a fatal blow to collective singing. Nowadays, group singing among adults is practiced only by a few minorities.

Foremost among these is the older generation, made up of persons who in their childhood practiced folk-singing; some of them, especially women, "continue" to sing in church. Even the in-between generation has shown itself partially sensitive to the call of the new liturgy for community singing: this is the sector cultivated by scouts, Catholic Action, and analogous movements which have taken hold of the habits of collective singing and turned them to new directions.

However, this is a limited phenomenon and has for the most part now been bypassed. Those sectors of the assembly which lay down strong conditions concerning the style of singing cannot serve as a certain basis and model for the singing of a heterogeneous community. It would be an anachronistic model. Even in these phases of its acculturation, the folklore cycle is closed and irreversible. Collective singing must not "continue"; it must be reborn.

In those countries where it exists, the twin structure school—church must not be overrated. It is not free of dangers: it tends to make choral singing appear as a model and an instrument of the constituted order, of the authoritarian establishment; moreover, it gives the liturgy a character of infantile regression.

Another series of conditions of a Scholastic origin on liturgical singing is posed by a bookish civilization. The educated faithful will usually feel offended in their cultural dignity if they are invited to repeat a brief refrain. They are disconcerted by the invitation to "acclaim"—that is, to "shout" a word or phrase;

[7] Cf. H. Hucke, "Musical Requirements of Liturgical Reform," in *Concilium 12* (New York, 1966), pp. 45-73.

they do this at the stadium, but school and books and musical etiquette always expressly forbade them from shouting. In short, they do not succeed in accepting the celebration as a proposal for community action which has an aspect of the unforeseen about it, as an experience in the field, an experiment which is here today and might not be here tomorrow: for them, liturgical singing—as the liturgy in general—is the execution of a written repertory already authenticated as "culture", already sanctioned as a rite. In a liturgy-as-feast he will weep for the liturgy-as-solemnity.

Lastly, we come to the young people. A liturgy-as-feast cannot be realized without the energetic and inventive contribution of youth. The revolution which they have effected in light music can instruct us concerning their strong points. Their song proposes a young action and style that are syntonic with contemporary culture, entirely oriented to the youthful dominant; the liturgy must ask itself whether its typologies on the contrary do not appear as decisively senile.

Youth singing is a model of rudimentary action on the part of a group; anyone can do the same thing as the others, but there are also the beginnings of differentiation of roles. This model is really "active" and inspires unity in action; this group is an animating group—which the liturgy needs in order to leaven the mass.

Is it a question of playing? Not a frivolous playing, in any case. It is a real feast in which no one becomes annoyed and in which rites are not repeated but one expresses oneself and realizes oneself. It is something serious, an obligation—and the "youth Masses" confirm this. The means of expression are typical of our age: a pre-musical song, an elementary antiartistic vocality, the expression of a culture which likes neither "fancy songs" nor "fine speeches"; in compensation, the resources of electronic technology are enlisted: amplifiers prolong our actions at will, freeing us from physical effort and create a resonant space, electrifying, stimulating and cathartic. And how can we fail to see that even the guitar is an immediate prolongation—

ductile and mobile—of human action which is part of man and act—much more than an organ affixed to a cold and far-off wall.

On the basis of their music the young people consolidate across the frontiers of race and language and class and culture. Is this not a model of brotherhood, of the *one liturgical voice?* In the final analysis, for youth it is not so much a case of melodies, art and musical notes, but of *sound*—that is, general climate and atmosphere. And sound is the very context of the life of young people who play and sing in the same style in which they speak and think and act. Even in the Christian celebration, what should interest us is not the music but the acting together by means of music.

Is a type of singing possible which would unite all these various voices of a composite assembly, or must we instead let each form express itself in turn in its own language?[8] Does it still make sense to retain a "people's song" which is in reality performed by a small minority, or is it better to leave collective singing for group celebrations in which there is greater probability of a unanimous expression?

VI
PLURALISTIC RECEPTION

If words are not received univocally, the addition of music transports us into a forest of diverse kinds of perceptions, and pluralism finds its greatest articulation. Here it is more inopportune than ever to fix norms; no one can say what type of reception will edify others.

Young people prefer sharp sounds, loud volume and rapid movements. Sharp sounds are perceived as higher in space,

[8] The two ways—a basic language and the use of languages differentiated according to cultural sectors—are examined in my book *L'acclamation. . .*, in the chapter "Langages et répertoires". Good suggestions concerning the first way are given in B. Huijbers, "L'art du peuple célébrant," in the collective work *La tâche musicale des acteurs de la célébration* (Paris, 1968); Italian ed.: *L'arte del popolo celebrante* (Torino-Leumann, 1968).

clearer and luminous; in turn, the loud volume of sound has the sense of affirmation, clarity, decision and importance. There is enough here to give us pause before terming such youth music as "secular".

On the other hand, the "religious adagio"—or, in general, music of the slow-grave-minor-organ type—provokes a whole gamut of ambiguous experiences: calm—recollection—weak lights (daybreak or dusk)—moderated sentiments—melancholy—nostalgia—sadness—expectation—mystery[9]—a "mystery" which is not precisely the paschal mystery, and a decidedly senile spirituality.

Musicians perceive things much differently than non-musicians. Yet in questions about music in church a great importance is still attributed to the opinion of musicians, forgetting the often much more useful opinion of sociologists, psychologists, pastors and the faithful.

The pluralism of the modes of reception has its principal source in the means of mass communication. It can be said that the radio, cinema and television form an immense kaleidoscope in which all repertories that are assimilable by the majority of the people revolve around contexts, presentations, and hence expectations and modes of reception that are practically infinite. The consequences are manifold.

A few ecclesiastics who are not very familiar with the mass media unreservedly consider as dance music what is simply everyday music and is found in dozens of diverse programs and situations—from the concert to the cinema to music to work by.

There is no reason to become alarmed at presumed dangers of alienation. The Christian assembly can make good use of them to aid concentration, lay emphasis on words and silence, create atmosphere adapted to the situation, and scan collective movements.

Such music is not an action of the assembly or any of its members; it is instead part of the atmosphere on the order of the architecture. Then it is not clear why even reproduced music

[9] Cf. R. Frances, *La perception de la musique* (Paris, 1958), p. 294.

(records and tapes), possibly even the electronic kind, cannot be used as background and commentary. The individual assemblies, individual groups, and the concrete implementation will dictate the realization of a sonorization favorable to the celebration instead of resonant spectacles.

VII
MUSIC AS CULTURE

Concert music implies direct reception. In the civilization of the mass media, music is also a fact of art and, more generally, a common cultural good to which one dedicates even a time of direct audition—though it may be minimal. It is therefore natural that even in church there is a minority that expects a cultural reception, the type of reception to which various centuries of "religious music" have accustomed Westerners.

The reception of art, which is as a rule something individualistic,[10] under certain conditions fosters a sense of socio-religious belonging. Let us take the case of Bach. The organ just about begins to play and immediately the cultured person recognizes that it is a fugue of Bach. It is Bach. It is our great music, the art of all ages, the true universal art. All of us grasp it without effort, yet it is highly instructive at the same time. This holds for Bach as well as for all the other great geniuses, great believers who have fused the religious ideal with art and vice versa. This is art at the service of the Church, and the Church as the patron of art. It is good to cultivate art; it is good to frequent the church. Every civilized man and every cultured person does so!

The implications of this "reassuring" and middle-class type of reception are: the liturgy as a *locus* of culture; Catholic triumphalism; conventional category of the religious as to genus and style; socio-cultural preferences of the liturgy; etc. A cultural elite could have this same experience with Palestrina or

[10] Cf. A. Silbermann, *Le musique, la radio et l'auditeur* (Paris, 1954), p. 152.

Gregorian chant; another elite would feel "reassured" by the presence of avant-garde music. As for light music, insofar as it is the cultural expression of the masses, it restores the traditional social balance, emphasizing the democratic aspect of the "Church of the poor".

VIII
Religious Folklore

For the middle- and lower-class "mass" culture, Palestrina and Gregorian chant are not, like Bach, a general cultural good regarded as something common, but rather a religious folklore and a spectacle which can be assisted at only in church. In effect, this music does not enter easily into the kaleidoscopic play of the mass media, and whenever it appears therein it is in unique reference to the "church" situation of its most evident—that is, external—aspect. We are confronted with a "sacred music" which comprises neo-Palestrinian or neo-Gregorian musical styles, liturgical recitatives, and the sound of the organ.

It is not through chance that the use of the organ has become quasi-exclusive in churches when an "objectively sacred" music was sought. Through its characteristics as a machine (inexpressivity, impersonality), it can very well refer symbolically to an immutable and unfathomable world: the world of the "divine". Once it has been established, the relation between the organ and the liturgy will remain immutable from the moment that the instrument becomes part of the church architecture and because its technology does not hold great surprises.

As for the recitative, we can note that it has been preserved by the liturgy for more than half a century after the disappearance of folk-singing, and when the recitative of the melodrama had already for a long time become a purely musical message.[11] Added to this is the fact that it was presented in conjunction with

[11] Cf. D. Carpitella, "Retrospettiva del cantastorie," in *Un secolo di canzoni* (Milan); A. Moles, *Théorie de l'information et perception esthétique* (Paris, 1958), pp. 183-87.

Latin, a dead language, whose liturgical function was no longer notional communication. The perception of the faithful, nowadays, is thus abundantly clear: the church recitative signifies solely the "sacred" understood as archaic and conventional. This evidently holds for all the present recitatives which in some way recall the traditional ones.

This alienating tendency on the part of the recitative is completely borne out in the "recto tono" where the word is mummified, interpersonal communication is congealed, and the liturgical action is petrified and dehumanized. Only a god of the dead could be pleased with such glacial homage, and the faithful who do not rebel on seeing the communitary expression enclosed in such a funereal apparatus probably believe not in the God of the rites but in the rites themselves.

It is surely convenient to retain this type of music and the relative expectation in which the presence of the "sacred" is indicated with absolute certainty, as is the case with ecclesiastical dress or the cross atop the steeple. But its ominous effects must also be pointed out. This church folklore which is now frozen and without life or power resembles a street signal, a simple word of warning. Uprooted from living culture, entirely "separated" from daily life, this music—or any music in such a conception— loses a great part of its expressive nature and becomes incapable of commenting on the situations of the assembly, or of becoming a sign of the living ecclesiastical structure.

IX

CONCLUSION

It would be wise in the future to avoid official "norms" in matter so radically relative as music and song. Here more than ever there is need to trust the Spirit, charisms, the local Church —above all, need to trust man. The ideal of a Mass in which all the rites which call for singing are in fact sung is a reasonable prospect, but a partial one and a swing toward formalism. No one can maintain that a Mass without song is less perfect than one with song. Rather, it is more just to encourage the "state of singing", the openness to expression, as a human condition favorable for celebration, for a liturgy-as-feast. But every Christian reunion must find its own paths toward a feast, to celebrate God in spirit and in truth, to *psallere sapienter*.[12]

[12] I am aware of the fact that the preoccupations with matters of practice in these pages have not allowed me to develop sapiential considerations which are of equal importance; for these I refer the reader to the excellent study of J. Gelineau, "Psallite sapienter," in the collective work already mentioned: *La tâche musicale des acteurs de la célébration, op. cit.*

Kilian McDonnell, O.S.B./*Collegeville, Minnesota*

Calvin's Conception of the Liturgy and the Future of the Roman Catholic Liturgy

I

ABUSES IN THE EARLY 16TH CENTURY

To understand Calvin's liturgical stance one would have to reflect on the abuses which in part typified liturgical life in the early 16th century. Among the abuses one could name raging objectivism (the exaggerated emphasis on *ex opere operato* effects of the sacraments, a one-sided concern not for sacramental sign and meaning but for efficacy; liturgical formulas need not be meaningful or understood, merely said; God understands Latin even though the people do not); the cultivation of false ultimates (the dislocation of the true eucharistic moment by the isolation of the consecration; the concentration of showing and seeing the body of Christ); ritualism (was it not a contemporary of Calvin, Teresa of Avila, who said that she would give her life for the right fulfillment of a rubric?; every word of the form must be carefully pronounced lest God be hindered from acting); the quantification of the liturgy (Masses, festal and votive, were multiplied so that "altarists", priests whose function was simply to say Mass, were numerous, with two churches in Breslau having 236 altarists between them; the proliferation of private Masses and of feasts); liturgical clericalism (the appropriation of worship by the true Israel, the clergy, while the people watched in reverent passivity from afar; the point of departure for eucharistic theologizing was the priest, not the worshiping community); the fixity of all liturgical forms (what is not commanded is forbidden; society and culture change but liturgical forms do not); and, finally, the neglect of preaching.[1] It is against this background that Calvin must be judged.

II

CALVIN'S LITURGICAL THOUGHT

When one considers the broad theological background of Calvin's liturgical thought, one notices that besides the christological dimension there was a strong pneumatological element, which corresponded to the character of his eucharistic doctrine. The immediate goal was christological—that is, union with Christ—and it is the Holy Spirit who effects this union,[2] an emphasis found also in Martin Bucer. Like the other reformers, Calvin has omitted an epiclesis for fear that it might be mistaken for a focal point substituting for the moment of consecration.[3]

Gerard van der Leeuw has suggested that Calvin's liturgical conception is basically Catholic and sacramental.[4] Whatever modifications one has to make in this thesis, the basic insight is correct. Calvin's intention, clearly stated, was to give an order which would be in accord with "the ancient Church of the apostles, martyrs and of the holy fathers".[5] If this is his model, it is not one Calvin felt obligated to imitate with servility. Liturgically, Calvin is a renovator rather than an innovator. Having once removed what he considered superstitions, his liturgical stance is characterized by conservatism. He wished to stand within the great liturgical tradition as long as the doctrine was orthodox and the service was heard and understood by the people.

[1] No attempt is made here to give a balanced account of the liturgical situation. What concerns us here are only some of the abuses against which Calvin was reacting.

[2] Cf. *Corpus Reformatorum* 9:773, 774 (hereafter cited as *CR*).

[3] Cf. G. MacGregor, *Corpus Christi* (London, 1959), p. 182.

[4] Cf. *Liturgiek* (Nijkerk, 1947), p. 151.

[5] *CR* 6:161.

The results of this renovation have been judged by Protestant scholars not to have been exceptional.[6] There is very good reason for the somewhat impoverished liturgy of Calvin. Calvin had to work within the context of the abuses mentioned above; like the other reformers his knowledge of liturgy was restricted almost entirely to the static and overburdened forms of the Roman rite; like the other reformers he appears to have known almost nothing of the Gallican and Eastern liturgies, and the knowledge he had of the primitive worship he was attempting to restore was meager and fragmentary, though he was a patristic scholar of some note.[7]

Calvin opted for a liturgical form which, in gesture and sign, was chaste and spare. Because of the neglect of preaching and the religious ignorance of the populace, Calvin, following Bucer, tended to be didactic and prolix in his ritual forms. The essential element of worship is doctrine: "The chief matter that the Lord enjoined upon us is to celebrate the mystery with true understanding. It follows, therefore, that the essential element lies in doctrine." [8] Though this came to be too intellectual an exercise where all is explained and everything is put into words, it must be said in Calvin's defense that doctrine, in Calvin, means the imparting of the Holy Spirit as well as instruction. However justified the accusations of didacticism might be, it must be admitted that Calvin conceived of the liturgy as a tool of evangelism (not revivalism), a converting ordinance, a dimension not much in evidence in Catholicism.

One of Calvin's pastoral liturgical norms is "edification of the Church".[9] It was within this context that he approached the problem of legislated and binding forms. During his first stay at

[6] Cf. J.-D. Benoit, *Liturgical Renewal* (London, 1958), pp. 29-30; W. D. Maxwell, *An Outline of Christian Worship* (London, 1936), p. 73; MacGregor, *op. cit.*, p. 182.

[7] A. Lecerf is almost certainly wrong when he suggests that Calvin perhaps had texts of the primitive liturgies before his eyes. Cf. *Etudes Calvinistes* (Paris, 1949), p. 46.

[8] *Opera Selecta*, eds. Peter Barth *et al.* (Munich, 1952-1962), 1:524.

[9] *Institutes of the Christian Religion*, IV, 10, 37 (hereafter cited as *Inst.*).

Geneva (1536-1538) he took the liberty to depart from Guillaume Farel's "La Manière et fasson", a procedure not at odds with Farel's own intentions. Both Farel and Calvin were using liturgical norms also found in Bucer, Zwingli and, to a minor extent, Luther. Zwingli was especially liberal in the matter of set forms. Bucer, who greatly influenced Calvin, contended in 1524 that except for the sermon, nothing should be dictated in the assembled congregation; everybody may pray and praise without restraint,[10] a position he pulled back from later because of the Anabaptist threat and Lutheran pressures. In these matters Calvin himself was more liberal in his enunciated principles than in practice, partly because he was temperamentally more concerned about the abuse of liberty than the defense of liberty. On the one hand he asserted that the liturgical forms are not "fixed and permanent sanctions by which we are bound".[11] He objected to "excessive attentiveness and caution" in following a fixed form as repugnant to freedom of conscience.[12] His concern here was for unity of doctrine and the edification and peace of the Churches, not pedantic conformity. "It is unworthy of us to introduce a servile conformity, which does not edify, into those things which the Lord has left to our liberty precisely for purposes of edification." [13] At the judgment we will not be examined on how exactly we have conformed, but on how we have used our liberty, how it has served edification. "Edification, that is the end to which our solicitude, our vigilance, our efforts, our application must tend." [14] Edification is not served by repetition. Fidelity to the form or divergence from it should depend on the necessities and diversities of time and place. Though one can change and institute new forms, insofar as it is expedient and for the edification of the Church, one should not think it necessary to create anew all that one wishes or wants for each service.

[10] Cf. "Grund und Ursach," in Martin Bucers Deutsche Schriften I (Gutersloh, 1960), pp. 241, 276-277.
[11] Inst. IV, 10, 31.
[12] Ibid.
[13] CR 6:5.
[14] Ibid.

"I admit that we ought not to charge into inovation rashingly, suddenly, for insufficient cause." [15]

A sobered Martin Bucer, in a series of pamphlets, put restraints on too great an exercise of freedom in the sacraments and public prayers.[16] Calvin, too, spoke of each minister "voluntarily imposing some necessity upon his freedom, insofar as this decorum of which we spoke or considerations of love shall require".[17] Set forms should be followed "without superstition, yet with a pious and ready inclination to obey; not to despise them not to pass over them in careless negligence".[18] The only place he provided for *ex tempore* prayer was before the reading and preaching of the Word, and even here Calvin, as Bucer, provided a model. Calvin was a liturgical conservative.

III
LITURGY AT VATICAN COUNCIL II

Since the 3rd and 4th century there has been no absolute liturgical freedom, and it is in this long liturgical tradition that Calvin stands. The norm for the future within Catholicism will be the norm Calvin enunciated: freedom within form. The whole attitude of the *Constitution on the Sacred Liturgy* toward rubrics in general, as well as the use *pro opportunitate* giving greater use of judgment on the part of the celebrant, stands in strong contrast to the objectified legislated performance demanded in the past. In the past newly ordained priests were taught that the personality of the priest should not break into the rite; he was to submerge himself in his role but never initiate a gesture or word which had not been legislated, certainly an expression of raging objectivism. The *Constitution on the Sacred Liturgy* is more concerned about forming interior attitudes in the celebrant which

[15] *Inst.* IV, 10, 30.
[16] Cf. G. J. Van de Poll, *Martin Bucer's Liturgical Ideas* (Assen, 1954, p. 24.
[17] *Inst.* IV, 10, 32.
[18] *Inst.* IV, 10, 31.

give authenticity to cultic gestures than giving orders on how he should hold his hands or how low he should bow. Greater attention will be given to the necessities and diversities of time and place. In contrast to the Tridentine reform, which was simply a codification of medievial rubrics concerning the priest (not the worshiping community), a codification which gave no attention to the size and character of the community, the future reforms will contend with a variety of celebrations in a variety of places [19]—for students in dormitory lounges, for workers in factory warehouses, for families in living rooms, as well as for the great undifferentiated crowd in the great cathedrals. The disagreement will continue between those who, on the one hand, see the liturgy as essentially a "givenness" handed down as law from the highest ecclesiastical authority, which yet allows for a degree of latitude, and those who, on the other hand, see liturgy not as a formula given from above but as the product of a living, worshiping community, which creates its forms out of the texture of its situation, with a regulatory function being exercised by the bishop and final approbation being given by Rome. A reform, however successful, which is a new law, fixing and freezing the forms which demand precise rubrical obedience, will certainly fail. Nothing in the contemporary cultural and sociological situation indicates that such a reform would be willingly received or could be successfully enforced. If society and culture change, does not the worshiping community change? Does not liturgy, which is the act of the worshiping community, change? The immobilism which set in during the early Middle Ages and was reinforced by the rubrical rigidity of the Council of Trent, can never be a viable solution, if it ever was. This is not to say that the fluidity of a liturgy created from below and approved from above does not have its own price.[20]

Part of the problem of form and freedom is the problem of tradition and translation. If one wishes to stand within the litur-

[19] Cf. *Constitution on the Sacred Liturgy*, nn. 37-40.
[20] Cf. "Some Problems of Liturgical Renewal," in *Ido-c*, Doss, 67-35, October 15, 1967.

gical tradition, as Calvin most certainly did, what concept of tradition is one going to adopt? Does one hand on to posterity exactly, in all details, what one receives from one's antecedents? Is this not to hand on static forms rather than living liturgy? Calvin felt no obligation to make such a conception of tradition his own. Or does one receive from history a body of constants which must be preserved but which are incarnated and transformed in terms of the worshiping community of a given place and time? The glories, so often extolled, of the Latin liturgy (brevity, sobriety, clarity, dignity, grandeur, fixity of form, a transhistorical objectivism, a supranational appeal) are not always, in every age and situation, qualities to be treasured. Is not fixity of form a dubious distinction when the same anaphora must serve the intellectuals of Brazilian college campuses and also the unlettered from the *favelas* of Rio de Janeiro? Is it not the supposed transhistorical character of the Roman liturgical forms, appealing to the universal man of every age, that makes them ill adapted to historically and sociologically varied mission situations? Obviously the resurrection of ancient prayers and rites is not enough. Even the much treasured Roman collects, treasured with good reason, do not always prove successful in translation. Contemporary translations of these prayers have shown that to some extent the medium was the message. In spite of the cadences and grandeur of these prayers, which thrilled the Latinist, frequently they become non-prayers in translation. They say nothing. And though Calvin's prayers were often didactic and prolix, they said something. Should the primary concern be the transmission of a culture and civilization of the past? Should prayers give expression to the cultural heritage and experience of the Church's past, or should the concern be to give expression to the experience of the Holy Spirit present in power, making Christ incarnate in the worship that a given community renders to the Father? There will be found some way to combine the glories of a living tradition with the power of a present Spirit. The true living tradition, not just a cultural heritage, is what must be preserved.

IV
CALVIN'S PRINCIPLE OF DOUBLE ACCOMMODATION

Implicit in Calvin's liturgical stance is the principle of double accommodation. He accommodated himself to the local liturgy and then accommodated the local liturgy to the needs of the congregation as he saw them.[21] He accommodated himself to Guillame Farel's liturgy when he came to Geneva, he accommodated himself to the liturgy which was largely Bucer's when he went to Strasbourg, and he again made the necessary accommodations when he introduced the Strasbourg liturgy in Geneva when he returned after his exile. He was critical in his approach to worship, and in every case he made those changes which he thought were demanded. These changes were made only in the light of the needs of "the state of the times" and because one worship form is not "suitable for all ages".[22] He was also capable of compromise, even though he saw that the compromise solution was not ideal. However, in this case, he publicly stated that certain liturgical customs were abnormal, and that he hoped posterity would return to a better observance.[23] That Calvin was forced to compromise by the magistrates—for instance, in the matter of the frequency of communion (he wished it every week, the magistrates four times a year)—should temper our judgment on Calvin's liturgical forms and practice. He was not entirely free, despite the myth that he was absolute dictator of Geneva. Indeed, were one to take Calvin at his liturgical best, one would have to choose his Strasbourg liturgy rather than his Genevan liturgy. He was more free in Strasbourg than in Geneva, although even in liberal Strasbourg he was also under some restrictions.

[21] Cf. E. Doumergue, *Jean Calvin*, Vol. 2 (Lausanne, 1902), pp. 499-502; *idem*, *Essai sur l'histoire du culte réformé* (Paris, 1890), p. 17.

[22] *Inst.*, IV, 10, 30.

[23] Cf. *CR* 17:311-312; 20:200-201.

V
TURNING AWAY FROM LITURGICAL CENTRALISM

Calvin's principle of double accommodation corresponds to the trend away from centralization of all liturgical initiative in Rome. For a thousand years the Holy See claimed the exclusive right in liturgical matters, and the claim was insisted upon with particular force after the Council of Trent, though there were some exceptions (the last missal of the diocese of Münster was issued without Roman approbation). The *Constitution on the Sacred Liturgy* represents a turning away from the liturgical centralism as expressed in Canon 1257. Without such a development there would have been no hope of the accommodation and adaptation of the liturgy to differing cultures and differing times. According to the *Constitution on the Sacred Liturgy* both individual bishops and national conferences of bishops have rights in matters which are specifically liturgical. There has been a certain historical basis for this development. The Roman Ritual was never made preceptive for the whole Church. The Ritual is essentially a book of the local Church. Local rituals remained in force, and in the last few decades new national rituals have been prepared by the national authorities and approved by the Holy See.

The restoration of a measure of liturgical competence to the local bishop will mean that the sociological pluralism will be reflected in a liturgical pluralism, a sociological pluralism which will mean that even within a given nation or diocese the liturgical situation will differ.[24] The pluriformity of liturgical practice which would flow from building worship forms on sociological pluralism would mean the end of a rigid conformity to a universal rite. At this point one must determine one's priorities. What has priority in a definition of liturgy: the sacred act of the

[24] Cf. H. Schmidt, "The Synod and Liturgical Renewal," in *Ido-c,* Doss. 67-40, November 2, 1967, pp. 1-3.

concrete assembly of God or a book of ritual forms? If the norms of the Roman tradition together with the accumulation of a wide range of contemporary liturgical experience are retained, the Roman liturgy would embrace a deeper unity in a worldwide plurality of forms. In the voluntary or gathered groups, such as one finds in the "underground church" and in the house-churches which one now finds organized within the parish structure, one could rightly expect a more domestic liturgy. These groups are formed by those who seek community relationships on a more human scale where true interpersonal relationships can be fostered. It is the nature of these gatherings to be less formal, more relaxed, but they are nonetheless serious in their religious aspirations. Indeed, it is the desire for true community and the desire for true religious experience which prompts their formation. Their unstructured, acephalous character, their fluidity and their domesticity demand liturgical forms which are less formal, less structured, more personal, intimate and immediate. This should not be interpreted to mean the death of true liturgy, but merely its accommodation from the great parish church to the simple living room of a given family.

For these and for other communities a meaningful liturgical expression can be achieved only by a certain controlled experimentation. That controls by competent authorities are still necessary and that a dynamic tradition is to be retained cannot be denied. What is insisted upon is that liturgy be the product of a living experience from below as well as legislation from above. On the other hand, the history of liturgy within some segments of Protestantism should act as a restraint. This history indicates what happens to liturgy when there are no controls, but only liberty, when there is no concept of a continuing liturgical tradition, but only the demands of the moment.[25]

[25] Cf. K. McDonnell, "Free and Formal Prayer in Protestant England," in *Worship* 40 (1966), pp. 472-82.

VI
CONCLUSION

Martin Bucer removed the words of institution from the Roman canon, the only part of the canon which Luther had retained. This he did in protest against the use of the words as a formula for transubstantiation. Calvin restored the words of institution, not as a formula, but as setting forth the promises, and as a form of preaching. The words are not directed to the elements but to persons.[26] One does not preach to bread. In baptism also there is no sacrament without preaching.[27] The words are directed not to the water but to persons.

There is no conceivable way one could construe the words of institution as found in the biblical text to mean a formula directed to the elements. Language is a social institution which demands involvement that elements cannot give. When a person speaks a word, he reveals meaning and also himself, and he rightfully expects a response which an element cannot give. The words of institution are no exception to the laws of language. The words were first spoken in a community to persons. It would be a hopeless distortion of the biblical text to think that Christ spoke the words as a formula, directing them to the elements. The words proclaim the death of the Lord to those whom the Word has called and gathered. Calvin's instincts here are theologically sound. The eucharist and baptism are also word, proclamation. On the pastoral level this would indicate a structuring and a celebration of the sacraments which would give expression to their character as effective proclamation, proclaiming signs; sacramental forms are not formulas directed to elements but proclamation directed to persons.

[26] Cf. Inst., IV, 17, 39.
[27] Cf. CR 45:126.

Jos Lescrauwaet, M.S.C./*Tilburg, Netherlands*

The W.C.C. and Liturgical Reform

All Churches are involved in liturgical reform, and none of them does this in isolation. Not only are all Churches subject to the general pressure that there should be more cooperation, but they are all challenged by the one basic question which affects the existence of every Church: What is the meaning of Christian worship in an increasingly secular world? Finally, in their study of the principles for a Christian worship, all Churches are finding out that there is clearly a universally valid basic structure. The constituent elements of this structure are the community of the faithful, the Word, the sacrament and its minister who is the servant of both Christ and the community. The recognition of these four elements not only blurs the theological contrasts between the Churches but also reinforces the original Christian view that these four elements must be expressed in the singular, in terms of a single supraeclesiastical reality: one community, one faith, one baptism, one bread and one authorized ministry. The mystery of worship reveals and expresses the mystery of the Church, and this mystery is one.

The liturgical dimension of ecumenism came out clearly in the Declaration of the Commission for Faith and Order about the unity of the Church at New Delhi (1961). The visible aspect of Christian unity was there described as the gathering of all those who are baptized in every place into one living community which exists in the one faith, proclaims the one Gospel, breaks the one bread, prays together, ministers together and is at the same time united with the whole Christian community everywhere and at all times, so that ministers and members are accepted by all, and if necessary can all act and speak together.[1] Since that Declaration the awareness that there may be various "ways of worship" but only one "Christian worship" has grown from strength to strength.

Montreal: 1963

The fourth world conference of the Commission for Faith and Order at Montreal in 1963 devoted two of its five sections to worship, one each to the universal and particular priesthood and the other to the nature of Christian worship.[2] These two sections not only show a remarkable consensus among the member Churches of the World Council but also an approach and climate of thought that look familiar to Catholics of today. It is true that this consensus is first of all represented by the theologians taking part in that Commission and the thirty-two delegates of the Montreal Conference who all together put their views to the Churches, but it deserves the attention of Catholic liturgiologists more than the various liturgical reforms attempted in local reformed Churches. The twenty pages devoted to this subject in the report show the results of expert study, achieved through the cooperation of all the great ecclesiastical traditions, the Eastern Orthodox included, which, for the first time in the history of Faith and Order, did not feel obliged to publish a separate declaration. One of the most striking points of this consensus lies in the section devoted to the eucharist which I am quoting here, partly because it was further elaborated in 1967 in Bristol:

"Despite many disagreements regarding holy communion and despite the desire of many for a fuller statement, we are drawn at

[1] Cf. *De Wereldraad van Kerken in New Delhi* (Utrecht, 1962), p. 133.

[2] Cf. *The Fourth World Conference on Faith and Order* (London, 1964), pp. 61-79.

least to agree that the Lord's supper, a gift of God to his Church, is a sacrament of the presence of the crucified and glorified Christ until he comes, and a means whereby the sacrifice of the cross, which we proclaim, is operative within the Church. In the Lord's supper the members of the body of Christ are sustained in their unity with their head and Savior who offered himself on the cross: by him, with him and in him who is our great high priest and intercessor we offer to the Father, in the power of the Holy Spirit, our praise, thanksgiving and intercession. With contrite hearts we offer ourselves as a living and holy sacrifice, a sacrifice which must be expressed in the whole of our daily lives. Thus united to our Lord, and to the Church triumphant, and in fellowship with the whole Church on earth, we are renewed in the covenant sealed by the blood of Christ. In the supper we also anticipate the marriage-supper of the Lamb in the kingdom of God." [3]

Because of the general appreciation of this statement and the increasing demand for intercommunion, the Commission for Faith and Order authorized its secretariat to organize a closer study of the eucharist at the meeting at Aarhus, Denmark.[4] At the request of the secretariat, J. J. von Allmen (Neuchâtel) wrote his *Notes on the Lord's Supper*.[5] This text, together with an essay by L. Vischer entitled *The Eucharist—Sign of Unity*,[6] served as a basis for discussion by some twenty theologians (Anglican, Lutheran, Presbyterian, Methodist, Orthodox and United Churches, as well as three Catholic ones) at Grandchamps in 1965. This dialogue produced a surprising unanimity, and a brief report was published for further study by some regional groups.[7] Both this report and the reactions of the regional study groups that were consulted were critically examined by

[3] *Ibid.*, pp. 73-74.

[4] Cf. *Aarhus Minutes* (Faith and Order Paper), n. 44, pp. 54-57.

[5] Later published with modifications as *Essai sur le repas du Seigneur* (Neuchâtel, 1967).

[6] Later published as "Questions on the Eucharist, Its Past and Future Celebration," in *Studia Liturgica* 5 (1966), pp. 65-86.

[7] *Study Encounter* 10 (1964), n. 2, and *Studia Liturgica* 5 (1966), pp. 121-25.

a special Commission of Faith and Order. This Commission drafted its recommendation in a report that was submitted to the plenary Commission of Faith and Order which met in Bristol in 1967. With a few minor amendments it was accepted and sent to the member Churches of the World Council for examination.

Bristol: 1967

The report on "The Holy Eucharist", accepted by the Bristol Conference, developed three points: (1) the character of the eucharist as an anamnesis and epiclesis, (2) the catholic character of the eucharist, and (3) eucharist and *agape*. Intercommunion was dealt with in an Appendix which offers no new points of view but rather new motives to come to a definite solution of this problem.

1. Christ instituted the sacrament of his body and blood, centered on the cross and the resurrection, as a memorial of God's total reconciliation in him. Christ himself is present in this memorial with his whole redemption so that the memorial is at the same time a foretaste of his return and the fulfillment of God's kingdom. It is not merely a matter of remembering the past or its significance but of Christ being active by means of the ecclesiastical celebration which therefore embodies both representation and anticipation. Through this communion with Christ the Church participates in this reality.

The re-presentation and anticipation through the anamnesis is realized in the thanksgiving and supplication where the Church is united with the Son, her great high priest. In the eucharist, Christ enables us to live and pray with him.

The anamnesis leads to the epiclesis because through his heavenly intercession Christ asks the Father to send the Spirit. On this basis the Church of the new covenant confidently prays for the coming of the Spirit that he may sanctify and renew her and lead her into all truth, and enable her to fulfill her mission in the world. Anamnesis, epiclesis and communion cannot be separated from each other. It is through the Spirit that Christ is made present and given us in our eucharist in the bread and wine.

Hence we draw the following conclusions:

(a) Since the memorial, the anamnesis, of Christ constitutes the very essence of both the eucharist and the preached Word, these two reinforce one another and must be administered in their mutual relationship;

(b) The memorial character of the eucharist should be expressed in both the anamnesis proper and the prayer of thanksgiving;

(c) The wording of the epiclesis in all liturgies should be such as to express a prayer for the descent of the Spirit on the People of God and at the same time a prayer for this descent on the whole eucharistic action, including the bread and wine. The consecration cannot be limited to a special moment in the service, and the placing of this epiclesis with regard to the words of consecration is of no decisive importance.

2. The catholic character of the eucharist is shown forth in every local celebration. The sharing of the one bread and the one cup in a given place shows forth the communion of the participants with the whole Christ and all those who participate in every place and at all times. The catholic Church is more than the sum of the local Churches and is fully shown forth in every local Church.

The catholic character is also evident in that every celebration ensures salvation and holds out the prospect of its fulfillment to all the world. However, this catholicity is blurred by the fact that the Churches cast doubts upon each other's celebrations. Insofar as a Church claims to be the manifestation of the universal Church, she has to show this in her pastoral and administrative regulations.

The catholicity of the eucharist implies an unavoidable summons to the Church to overcome all division, whether national, racial or confessional. Since the Church is Christ's body for all mankind, she is subject to a great diversity of cultural and social situations. The local Churches should therefore respect the differences between themselves. At the same time they should avoid everything that might give rise to misunderstanding, mutual alienation or division.

3. The celebration of the *agape* is characterized as a communal meal which takes place explicitly in the name and the presence of Christ and which gives concrete expression to the responsibility for each other as well as for the world.

The Churches are exhorted to show above all this *agape* aspect of the eucharistic celebration in such a way that every one can recognize in the eucharist the highest expression of Christian brotherly love. *Agape* celebrations can serve to strengthen community awareness, including a sense of joy as well as a sense of responsibility, if they are seen as related to the eucharist.

Occasionally the *agape* can be celebrated without being preceded or followed by the eucharist, in order, for instance, to stimulate communal life or concern for present needs, but care must be taken that this does not lead to underrating the eucharist, let alone to a confusion of *agape* and eucharist.

Interdenominational celebrations of the *agape* could help to express Christian solidarity and Christian witness. Every community of any denomination should therefore first celebrate its own eucharist and then proceed to an *agape* celebration with other Christians.

The Bristol Conference report concludes with the recommendation that a report should be drafted which gives a comprehensive view of the growing ecumenical consensus in this matter of the eucharist. A popular edition of this should inform the general public of these developments.[8]

The limited scope of this article does not allow a detailed comparison of these documents with the relevant ones of Vatican Council II, but such a comparison would show a strikingly positive result and show that here and there there is almost literal agreement in the texts.

[8] Cf. *New Directions in Faith and Order—Bristol 1967* (Faith and Order Paper), n. 50, pp. 60-68, 141-43.

Uppsala: 1968

This Assembly of all the Churches of the World Council devoted one of its six sections to "Worship in a Secular Age". The choice of this theme originated in the widespread tension between the various practices of Christian worship and the modern view of the meaning of human life with its resulting corresponding mentality. The schema for the discussion divides the problem into three aspects:

1. Secularization as a call to renewal. A positive assessment of secularization as an historical process where the real potentialities of man and world are recognized leads to a new view of the reality of God, man and the world. As Jesus Christ manifests the reality of God, establishes the reality of man and shows the potentiality of this world, he is not only the norm and condition of true worship but also the one who makes us capable of this worship.

2. The living tradition of worship. The universality of Christ's priesthood creates a real continuity in ecclesiastical worship regardless of time, culture and situation. Word and sacrament are directed to the actual communication between God and man, and so both these elements must be constantly attuned to the contemporary mind.

3. The implications of secularization for the renewal of the tradition. The Churches should teach their members to pray in a way that is both authentic and understood. The basic attitude in worship and prayer should be imparted to the children by the family. Both public and personal worship should incorporate the issues that are actually alive in the world. Prayers should allow for change and different ways of formulation. At the same time Christians should know how to pray within themselves, in silent love and worship. Finally, both communal and personal prayer remain subject to attack by powers hostile to God, powers that disintegrate, discourage and divide. This aspect, too, should be brought out in Christian worship.[9]

[9] Drafts for Sections—Uppsala 1968 (Geneva, 1968), pp. 96-111.

I finished this article before I could avail myself of the official reports of the World Assembly at Uppsala. But the eighteen theses which served as a guide for the discussion outline a task which could lead to a far-reaching renewal, and this renewal might well lead to a new and communal approach to Christian worship. Even here, however, the directives, though approved by the plenary assembly, will not be enough for the decisions that determine the liturgical reform needed for each Church. Moreover, the proposals put forward by the World Council in no way render individual initiative superfluous, and the most promising factor here is the Societas Liturgica.

The Societas Liturgica

This association came into being at a conference called for this purpose, and was attended by some fifty liturgiologists —Anglican, Baptist, Lutheran, Catholic, Methodist and Orthodox, from Europe, North America and Australia. This Conference was already prepared by the meetings at Grandchamps (1965) and Strasbourg (1965), and indirectly by the international ecumenical periodical *Studia Liturgica* since 1962. The founder-members met as individual liturgical experts, but more than half proved to belong to national or confessional liturgical commissions, so that contact with the authorities was ensured. Metropolitan Emilianos was, moreover, present as representative of the World Council together with various members of the study group of the Commission for Faith and Order.

The aim of the Society is to promote the study of liturgical and related subjects, including the pastoral consequences of such a study, to facilitate the exchange of the results of this study and other liturgical ideas, to encourage a deeper mutual understanding of the various liturgical traditions, and to search for ways and means to convince the modern world of the importance of worship.

The Society proposes to proceed on three lines: to organize world conferences, to organize smaller study groups or more limited conferences, and to promote publications that serve the aims of the Society. The first world conference is planned for 1969 and will discuss the theme "Our Language in Worship— Revision, Renewal and Development". In view of this, informative surveys have been circulated regularly since 1967, particularly about the liturgical language in the Catholic, Anglican, Swedish and other traditions.

Membership is open to whoever teaches or studies liturgical and related matter, is active in official liturgical commissions and has made important contributions to the liturgical life of the Churches, as well as anyone else whom the Society wishes to invite. The membership list shows that all important centers for liturgical study and action are represented, at least insofar as the West is concerned. Most prominent are the Catholics, Lutherans, Presbyterians and Anglicans or Episcopalians. The list also contains the names of very many well-known experts.[10]

Prospects

As in the Catholic Church, so in the reformed Churches the movements for liturgical renewal sprang from individual initiatives. Their development seems to coincide in most cases with the origin of the ecumenical movements in those Churches. Both types clearly derive from that new ecclesiastical awareness which they have in common. Both passed through very similar phases: first a romantic interest in the past, then historical investigations, followed by a period of interest in biblical theology, and finally, today, the interest in the problems created by the new approach to the relations of the Church with the world. In the meantime, these individual initiatives have been taken over by ecclesiastical authorities which have embodied the responsibility for both the liturgical and ecumenical developments in their program.[11]

The most important aspects of this growing liturgical reform are therefore not the numerous instances where the reformed Churches have adopted elements with which we as Catholics are

[10] The Secretariat's address is G. Mayes, The Deanery, Lismore, Co. Waterford, Ireland.
[11] Cf. J. Lescrauwaet, *Liturgisch Woordenboek* II (Roermond, 1966).

familiar. The important fact is rather that the reformed Churches
see worship increasingly as an essential part of the Church's life,
and here they are aware of the tension between historical origin
and continuity on the one hand and the renewal postulated by
modern life and modern thought on the other. This growing
awareness puts them on the same road as that pursued by Catholicism so that we are making the same discoveries. There is a
growing consensus about the nature of Christian worship, particularly about the relation between Word and sacrament, between the ecclesiastical and the eucharistic body of Christ,
between the communal and the individual *diakonia,* between
Christian unity and pluriformity, and between the internal and
the outward expression of Christian worship. This growing agreement gradually finds outward expression in words and rites, in
atmosphere and in every kind of liturgical activity. For some the
process is too gradual, but the progress of this converging
understanding of the faith is in any case most promising. It offers
far better guarantees than the occasional and incidental changes
brought about in the ritual. On the other hand, the growing
secularization of our age should goad all the Churches into a
little more courageous approach to this reform of the liturgy.

Colin Buchanan/*London, England*

Liturgical Reform in Anglicanism

The Anglican Communion is a heterogeneous family of 19 autonomous Churches or Provinces (and several extra-provincial dioceses), all springing from the Reformation in the British Isles. The only logical definition of the family is that it consists of those Churches which have bishops who are invited by the archbishop of Canterbury to the decennial Lambeth Conference (last held in 1968), for there is no constitutional connection between them. Each episcopate is historically traceable to the bishops of the English or Irish Reformation, and while the Thirty-Nine Articles are hardly a living bond today, there is one common inherited liturgical ethos which still characterizes Anglicanism. If the doctrinal features of the ethos have been more open to change than the accoutrements (e.g., surplices and "New Cathedral" chanting), that is an oddity predictable in an odd institution. Clearly, the Anglican Communion is not to be confused with the Church of England, and in many liturgical changes (good and bad) the initiative has been taken by the younger Churches. The Lambeth Conferences themselves have played a part in changes, although their findings possess not a conciliar, but only a moral force. Until 1920 they rather deprecated alterations in the 1662 Book of Common Prayer, from 1920 to 1948 they cautiously approved the prin-

108

ciple of change, and in 1958 the relevant subcommittee heartily recommended the principle and made detailed proposals affecting all the main services.[1] The 1968 Conference did not tackle liturgy.

Nevertheless, the Church of England itself does have a very distinctive place. There are several reasons for this. It is still the Church of the English nation, and therefore includes 26 million baptized English men and women (though perhaps only 10% of these are even Easter communicants). It thus ranks as theoretically larger than the whole of the rest of the Anglican Communion put together. The archbishop of Canterbury has a special position as chairman of the Lambeth Conference. The scholarship of the Church of England carries great weight elsewhere. The English missionary Societies (including lesser support from Ireland, Scotland and Wales) provide about 70% of the whole overseas missionary force of the Anglican Communion, and this helps to keep attention directed toward England. The tension between Catholic and Evangelical is felt most acutely in England, which gives an added significance to decisions taken there. Finally, the Book of Common Prayer originated in England, and this has led to special attention (and in some cases a special constitutional status) being accorded to revision in England. Thus particular attention is given here to England itself, and the writer, as a member of the Archbishops' Liturgical Commission since 1964, has at that point firsthand experience of the course of revision.

I
The Background to Liturgical Revision

Anglican worship derives from Cranmer's drastic (but necessary) reforms of 1549 and 1552. Minor further changes were

[1] For the effect of these on eucharistic liturgy, see C. O. Buchanan, *Modern Anglican Liturgies* (Oxford, 1968), Ch. 2.

made in 1662 after the restoration of the monarch and epis-
copacy in 1660. Since then the 1662 Book of Common Prayer
has remained the only legal book of worship in the Church of
England right up until 1966, and it has traveled around the
world as (second only to the Bible) a foundation document in
practically all plantings of Anglicanism elsewhere. There were revisions of it in the 18th century when first Scotland (1764) and
secondly (and derivatively) America (1790) adopted new eucharistic rites, but there was little other change anywhere until
1900. Indeed many Churches (e.g., England, Wales, Ireland,
Canada, Uganda, C.I.P.B.C.,[2] Australia and New Zealand) retained 1662 virtually unchanged up into the last decade.

The phrase "the only legal book" reflects the Book's enforce-
ment in the Church of England by the 1662 "Act of Uniformity". This required a scrupulous adherence to the textual
and ceremonial directions in the Book, and no priest, parish,
diocese or synod had any authority to alter the forms, and no
substantial proposals for change were again put before Par-
liament until 1927-8 (and then they were unsuccessful). The
Act of Uniformity thus conferred on the Book an indefinite im-
munity from revision, and this created a liturgical stability verg-
ing on ossification.

In the last century patterns of Sunday worship have changed.
Around 1900 these were roughly as follows: evangelical and
"central" churchmen had a said 8 A.M. communion service,
without either sermon or hymns. At 11 A.M. they had morning
prayer (or Matins) with sermon, and at 6:30 P.M. they had
evening prayer (or Evensong) with sermon. A large proportion
of the regular worshipers rarely or never receive communion.
Anglo-Catholics (a product of the 19th century) insisted both
that communion should be received fasting, and also that the
eucharist was the great service of the day. Hence their pattern
was a said 8 A.M. Communion (for the sake of communicants),
followed by an 11 A.M. High Mass, with sermon but probably

[2] Church of India, Pakistan, Burma and Ceylon.

without communion. Thus at both ends of the ecclesiastical spectrum the Word and the sacrament were sundered, and those who
only attended Church once on a Sunday would receive one or
other but not both. Anglo-catholics were also starting to imitate
post-Tridentine Roman practice by reserving the sacramental
elements (in defiance of the law) and introducing extra-liturgi-
cal devotions to them. In the liturgy itself the Roman canon
would be inserted silently, while the whole service would be accompanied by full Roman ceremonial. The celebrant's part was
to "do" the liturgy with scrupulous "correctness", while the worshipers were urged to rely upon their manuals of private devotions. At the same time evangelical worshipers found their closest
approach to God in *ex tempore* prayer meetings and in personal
piety, while the public liturgy (that is, morning or evening
prayer) became the background to the sermon, and sometimes
only that. Thus, ironically, both ends of the spectrum were again
alike—this time in sundering the liturgy from private devotions.
Individualistic devotion was no doubt running strong, but the
unity of the people of God, as expressed, focused and sustained
in the liturgy, was not apparent. These patterns were duly ex-
ported, and Victorian Anglo-catholicism is still to be found in
the West Indies, while Victorian evangelicalism is particularly
obvious in Uganda.

A Liturgical Movement in the Church of England first took
definable form in the 1930s. It was fostered by two books of the
Anglo-catholic monk, Gabriel Hebert: *Liturgy and Society*
(1935) and *The Parish Communion* (1937). Since then there
has been a progressive move among all, except the very cautious,
toward the reintegration of Word and sacrament and a making
of liturgy relevant, intelligible, and corporate. The "parish communion" is a 9:30 A.M. or 10 A.M. celebration of the eucharist
for the whole congregation. A sermon is preached. All take part
in the singing, the prayers and the responses. Selected laity often
read lessons, bring forward the sacramental elements and, less
frequently, lead the intercession. Virtually all communicate, ex-

cept the young children (who are nevertheless present). Ceremonial is simplified, and many celebrants take a westward position to foster the sense of the corporate.[3] Evangelicals have been slow to adopt the parish communion, being loath to abandon their traditional framework for preaching the Word of God, but they do tend now to have at least one morning or one evening main service a month that includes a corporate celebration of communion with a sermon.

Both the current patterns spelled out above are open to objection. Evangelicals are clearly still in a state of transition. They may arrive at some more permanent solution, since 1,000 of them, at their Congress at Keele in 1967, stated: "We determine to work toward the practice of a weekly celebration of the sacrament as the central corporate service of the church." [4] Equally, the parish communion movement is encountering obstacles of which its own exponents are often unaware. Large communion services mean lack of time, and preaching is the first casualty. At the same time the concentration upon one main service tends to run down evening prayer. This then becomes unattractive both to that (small) proportion who currently attend worship twice on a Sunday, and also to outsiders and inquirers who are more likely to look for a non-sacramental service.

The parish communion is now found around the world (though least in Evangelical areas). However the Anglican Communion has a great shortage of clergy in South America, Africa and Asia, and it may thus be impossible to provide a weekly communion service in many congregations. Catechists often lead non-sacramental services, and there is a slow swing over to antecommunion (rather than morning or evening prayer) discernible in such circumstances. The problem of part-time or spare-time clergy is focused by this need, and various experimental patterns of ministry may be expected to emerge in the younger Churches in the coming years.

[3] This practice, which normally involves moving the Table out from the East wall, is traceable to the late 1940s, but its popularity is a phenomenon of the 1960s.

[4] *Keele '67* (London, 1967), para. 76.

II
GENERAL TRENDS IN LITURGICAL REVISION

New patterns and varying local needs have led to a new constitutional set of procedures for authorizing forms of worship—i.e., the concept of "experimentation". In 1549, 1552 and 1662 revised liturgies were written down first, and then imposed without ever having been used. Even the abortive English 1927-8 revision was similar. But in the 1960s services have been given only "experimental" authorization. They are only alternatives to the statutory services, and thus, although they stretch the concept of uniformity, they do not imperil the unique doctrinal status of the existing Book of Common Prayer, nor can any minister be compelled to employ them. They usually have only a brief period of life accorded them. Such new canonical procedures have recently been adopted by England, Wales, Ireland, Canada, America, Australia and New Zealand, among others. Experimentation with responsible review should prove a safeguard against renewed ossification.

The 1960s have also seen the wholehearted participation of Evangelicals in liturgical revision. 1662 is a Protestant Book, which has meant that wherever new Anglican Churches or Provinces have been founded (beyond the writ of the Act of Uniformity) Anglo-catholics have hastened to revise the eucharistic rite, and often the baptismal and burial ones also. Evangelicals, on the other hand, until recently have seen no reason to revise 1662. This has allowed Anglo-catholics all the initiatives in revision, and had by 1960 apparently established a solid trend in all overseas revisions. By then the 20th century had seen 17 new eucharistic rites in the Anglican Communion, of which at 12 were wholly inspired by Anglo-catholics,[5] and the

[5] Swahili Mass (1919), Bombay (1922), N. Rhodesia (?1925), America (1928), Nyasaland (?1929), S. Africa (1929), Scotland (1929), Ceylon (1933), Korea (1938), Madagascar (1945), Japan (1959), West Indies (1959). These are all printed in B. Wigan, *The Liturgy in*

other five partially so.[6] But since 1960 the situation has been reversed. The four years 1964-7 saw 15 further new eucharistic rites, of which only four have a definitely Anglo-catholic basis,[7] three more show signs of Anglo-catholic influence,[8] two are roughly neutral [9] and six are broadly Protestant.[10] There is thus now no one trend, and individual Churches are free from any pan-Anglican pressures which were building up a decade ago.

Another new feature of the 1960s, which is currently under hot debate, is the problem of liturgical English. Until 1960 this was no problem. However contemporary the vernacular might be in Mataco or Swahili, the English tongue was, for liturgical purposes, unchanged since Cranmer, and apparently unchangeable. The very genius of Cranmer's work left the sad entail of a linguistic stagnation, with apologists seeking rationalizations similar to those thrown up in defense of Latin in the Mass. Even at the time of writing, the rock of Cranmer's Tudor English is only crumbling very slowly. But there are now visible changes from rolling periods into short coordinate sentences, from verbosity into brevity, from archaic words into modern speech, and, in particular (though certainly not most important) from "thou" into "you" in the address to God. The lead has been given in Australia and New Zealand, but new proposals in England in 1968 go beyond the advances made in the Antipodes.

A slow trend toward ecumenical liturgy should also be noted, a trend prompted by the Church of South India liturgy of 1950.

English (Oxford, 1964), except the Madagascar rite which is in Buchanan, *op. cit.*

[6] England (1928), Hong Kong (1938 and 1957), Canada (1959) and C.I.P.B.C. (1960). These are all printed in Wigan, *op. cit.*, except the Hong Kong rite, of which the 1957 text is in Buchanan, *op. cit.*

[7] America (1967), Brazil (1967), Scotland (1966), Wales (1966). All these are printed in Buchanan, *op. cit.*

[8] England *First Series* (1966), Hong Kong (1965), *A Liturgy for Africa* (1964). All these are printed in Buchanan, *op. cit.*

[9] England *Second Series* (1967), New Zealand (1966). These are printed in Buchanan, *op. cit.*

[10] Australia *A Modern Liturgy* (1966), Chile (1967), East Africa Union Liturgy (1966), Iran (1967), Ireland (1967), Nigeria Union Liturgy (1965). All these are printed in Buchanan, *op. cit.*

Two Anglicans, Dr. L. W. Brown and Rev. T. S. Garrett, were influential in its compilation, and each has had a hand in another ecumenical liturgy since. In East Africa Dr. Brown played a part in the producing of a union liturgy in which Lutherans were involved, while in Nigeria T. S. Garrett helped to ensure that the Nigeria union liturgy followed the CSI liturgy extremely closely. Both these union liturgies have been authorized by the Anglicans in the respective areas, although neither union has been consummated. In England a joint liturgical group (not including Roman Catholics) has produced a set of calendar and lectionary proposals for Sundays, and this too may well soon be adopted by the Church of England. In other countries (e.g., America, Canada, North India, etc.) union negotiations are under way, and ecumenical liturgy is to be expected in time. It is probable that only in such unions will the liturgy divest itself of its peculiarly Anglican (and sometimes pan-Anglican) guise and root itself thoroughly in the soil of its local culture.

III

REVISION OF THE EUCHARIST

Gregory Dix' book *The Shape of the Liturgy* (1945) has been a turning point in revision of the eucharist. His prescription was a "fourfold" shape, corresponding to our Lord's taking, giving thanks, breaking and distributing. The "taking" he saw as worked out in the offertory of the elements, and it is his influence which has restored this to a position immediately before the canon. Similarly the breaking is now separated from the canon as the third of the four actions, and the four actions all come in fairly close sequence. Dix' insistence that the canon is a thanksgiving has released modern revisions from the old debates about the "moment" of consecration. "Western" Anglo-catholics have always asserted that the narrative of institution consecrates, while in the 1920s and 1930s the Hippolytean text led many scholars to insist that the epiclesis was the primitive form (an idea which had earlier been found in the Scottish and American rites). There were great debates in England and South Africa about the "moment" in the 1920s, and the South African Synod even then declared that the essence of consecration was thanksgiving. Dix, however, popularized this notion, which grew not from his reasoned rejection of the epiclesis but from his insistence that the eucharistic prayer was originally a thanksgiving, as his "shape" required. Lambeth 1958 added its weight to this view. Thus the epiclesis is now absent (except in linear descendants of the 18th-century rites), and the mood in revision is a new emphasis on thanksgiving, found in long Prefaces, ascriptions of praise opening the post-Sanctus, corporate responses to the narrative, thanksgivings in the anamnesis, and full doxologies. Manual acts have been pruned, but "Western" ideas still have a foothold in the normal provisions for supplementary consecration. There is perhaps a growing uncertainty as to what consecration *is*.

At other points there have been generally agreed changes in structure, largely made to sharpen the division of the service into an antecommunion (or ministry of the Word) and a communion (or ministry of the sacrament). Three lessons interspersed by canticles lead to first the sermon, then the Creed, then intercessions designed for congregational participation. The confession and absolution are still in the communion proper in England and Ireland, but elsewhere have been moved to the very beginning of the antecommunion. The postcommunion has been lightened by the moving of the Lord's Prayer into the sacramental "shape" itself, and by moving the *Gloria in excelsis,* which Cranmer placed at the end, back to the beginning of the service after the penitential opening.

The revisions have raised various doctrinal problems. One is the content of sacrifice. 1662 laid great weight upon our Lord's "full, perfect, and sufficient sacrifice, oblation and satisfaction" being offered on Calvary. There is a mood abroad that would lighten that weight, and this has had its effect on texts, particularly in England. Another problem surrounds our response to our Lord's command: "Do this." What do we in fact do? Cranmer said we eat and drink (and did it immediately after the narrative which ends with the command). Anglo-catholics desire to return to the traditional anamnesis containing an oblation. Evangelicals, while not objecting to the return of an anamnesis, have insisted that its content must not be an explicit oblation, which is *not* what our Lord commanded—hence the return in England and elsewhere to language such as "we make the memorial", which leaves the problem temporarily unresolved. The third problem surrounds petitions for the departed, which again Evangelicals, looking not only to Cranmer but also to Scripture, have opposed, and again compromise texts have been found. The present writer had to dissent from the England eucharistic proposals in 1966 over both these last two points, and that hastened the quest for compromises.

One of the most interesting features of the revision of texts has been the growth of a family of rites with little connection with England at all. The CSI Liturgy of 1950 reappears almost verbatim in the Nigeria union liturgy (1965), and only slightly altered in the Iran liturgy (1967). It lies behind the Lambeth 1958 proposals, and these in turn have been worked out by Dr. Brown himself in *A Liturgy for Africa* (1964), designed for all the African Provinces. This in turn lies behind the East Africa union liturgy (1966) and the New Zealand liturgy (1966). CSI has also had some effect on the Irish liturgy (1967) and the Australian *A Modern Liturgy* (1966); the latter is distinctive in having separate thanksgivings for the bread and for the cup. This is perhaps one further indication that pan-Anglican uniformity is disappearing.

IV

THE REVISION OF BAPTISM/CONFIRMATION

Space will only allow here for the spotlighting of certain problems. A controversy has raged since the 1890s as to whether confirmation is a purely domestic pastoral ordinance, or a separate dominical sacrament on its own, or the completion of a complex sacrament (water and the imposition of hands) of initiation. The last of these views (propounded by Mason, Dix, Thornton, etc.) has been slightly predominant in the texts, and is followed frequently in practice where the bishop administers adult baptism, confirmation and first communion all at one service (as the experimental texts allow, or even expect). The other great problem is infant baptism. There is uncertainty as to whether it has any warrant at all, how far it should be administered "indiscriminately", and whether the declarations of repentance and faith can properly be made by proxy. The texts vary on all these points, the only signs of a consensus at all being a slow awareness that all baptisms should take place at main public services, and not at the traditional English "4 o'clock". The growing secularization of the English-speaking world is posing problems for infant baptism which the liturgists do not feel able to solve purely in the realm of liturgy.

Anglicans of the future will thus have even greater problems to tackle. When should the baptized child of believers become a communicant? And what should the Church do for the child of unbelievers? There are as yet no clear answers to these questions.

PART II
BIBLIOGRAPHICAL
SURVEY

Heinrich Rennings/*Trier, West Germany*

What Is the Liturgy Supposed To Do?

I n n. 21 of the *Constitution on the Sacred Liturgy,* Vatican Council II expressed the wish that "a general restoration of the liturgy should be undertaken with great care". In this statement and, in fact, the whole of the Constitution the highest authority in the Church took up the desire for a reform of worship which had developed during the last decades and extended the partial reforms undertaken by the popes of this century to a general reform of the liturgy. This led to a deeper theological understanding of the liturgy and laid the foundation for a view of the Church's worship which differed on many points from that of the post-Tridentine period. It rang in a new phase of the development of the liturgy in the Western Church.

The question arises, then, whether the conciliar decision in favor of a comprehensive reform of the Church's worship and the Council's concept of the liturgy also has consequences for "liturgy" as a branch of theology which deals with the scientific study of worship.

Is it enough for this study simply to add the *Constitution on the Sacred Liturgy* (and other conciliar documents), the demands for the application of this Constitution and the new liturgical books to the already existing study material and to treat all this with the same method that up until now prevailed in such matters? Does the study of the liturgy still fulfill its task as a theological discipline in the present phase of Church history if it proceeds on the same lines as in the past? Is this the responsible service which it owes to the Church and her religious assemblies today and in the future? What should be its aim, and what should it do to achieve this aim? What are the points on which a post-conciliar study of the liturgy should concentrate, and what is its scope? What is the place of the study of liturgy in relation to the other branches of theology and what are its connections with other branches of science? To answer these questions I would like to suggest a few key points which might be of interest to people outside the narrow circle of professional scholars. It might be useful to begin with a brief methodical but not chrono-logical survey of what the study of liturgy saw as its purpose since it began to flourish in the last century.

The Various Ideas about the Task of the Study of Liturgy

The scientific and theological study (genuine or claimed as such) of worship obviously depends in large measure on the way people think of liturgy in a given age, and this leads to various opinions and surprisingly different approaches to what is con-sidered the proper material for such a study.[1]

1. Where liturgy was seen mainly as a collection of rules and regulations laid down by the hierarchy for the establishment of public rites and ceremonies, the study of liturgy meant almost exclusively the systematic treatment and interpretation of these rules and regulations. In this case the study of liturgy (*scientia liturgica*) was the same as the study of rubrics.[2] The textbooks for a liturgy understood in this way were books which described in detail the outward procedure of the rites. Apart from the liturgical books themselves, the most quoted sources were signifi-

[1] A survey of these approaches may be found in C. Vagaggini, *Theologie der Liturgie* (Einsiedeln, 1959), pp. 9-12; P. Oppenheim, *Introductio in scientiam liturgicam* (Turin, 1940), pp. x-xix; A. G. Martimort, "L'enseignement de la Liturgie dans les séminaires," in *Seminarium* 19 (1967), pp. 107-29; E. Bartsch, *Liturgiewissenschaft: Was ist Theologie?* (Munich, 1966), pp. 310-49; B. Botte, "A propos des manuels de liturgie," in *Questions liturgiques et Paroissiales* 33 (1952), pp. 117-24.

[2] Cf. F. X. Coppin and L. Stimart, *Sacrae Liturgiae Compendium* (Tournai, ³1905), p. 2.

cantly the innumerable decisions and replies that came from the Congregation of Rites (there are 4,000 items in the *Decreta authentica*) which grew into a veritable jungle of casuistry. This view would naturally see the study of liturgy as a subdivision of the study of Canon Law.[3] This complicated and involved system of rubrics, of which a vice-general relator of the Congregation of Rites said at the time that "not even the cleverest rubricist could disentangle the threads anymore",[4] created a whole class of interpreters and commentators to deal with the laws laid down for the liturgy. Criticism was directed not so much against their particular labor which was found to be indispensable in those days as against the identification of the study of liturgy with rubricism. The knowledge of rubrics was declared to be either an auxiliary science to the study of liturgy or simply made part of the practical formation of the clergy.[5]

2. For others the main point in the study of liturgy was the evaluation of the Church's worship in the light of its historical development. For them the liturgy consisted in the "acts" and "forms" of worship which had been molded by many and varied influences in a process of centuries. The firm emphasis on the historical elements and the rich data provided by historical research made some liturgical scholars consider the *history of liturgy* as the principal object of the study of liturgy.[6] Here the general climate of a strong, historically-colored view of science may have influenced the situation, because liturgical scholars concerned about the scientific justification and autonomy of their subject welcomed the support provided by historical research.[7]

[3] A. Vigourel, *Manuel de Liturgie* (Paris, [3]1921), p. 7; C. Callewaert, *De S. Liturgia universim* (Bruges, [3]1933), p. 175.

[4] J. Löw, in his Foreword to J. Pfab, *Kruze Rubrizistik* (Paderborn, 1958), p. 5.

[5] V. Thalhofer and L. Eisenhofer, *Handbuch der katholischen Liturgik* I (Freiburg, [2]1912), p. 56.

[6] Cf. C. Vagaggini, *op. cit.*, p. 9: "While the study of liturgy was at first mere rubricism, today it is almost universally treated as an historical subject."

[7] Thalhofer and Eisenhofer, *op. cit.*, I, p. 183: "The only possible way for a development of the study of liturgy is that of Probst"; but, a little before this statement, the authors say that Probst had exclusively concentrated on the "historical aspect".

The history of liturgy, as it is still called, for instance, in a well-known theological lexicon of recent date, was not merely the indispensable foundation but "an essential element of the study of liturgy".[8] Nobody will deny the necessity of historical research for the liturgy, but the fact that some people thought the study of liturgy was an historical discipline and so was a sub-division of history, particularly Church history,[9] shows to what exaggeration this opinion could lead. The most blatant example of this too exclusively historical view of the liturgy remains the lexicographic work of F. Cabrol and H. Leclerq which began publication in 1907 under the significant title of *Dictionnaire d'archéologie chrétienne et de liturgie*—as if liturgy has any closer links with archeology than any other theological discipline.

This exaggeratedly historical view of liturgy [10] and the consequent ranging of the study of liturgy under the heading of Church history were rejected on the basis of a more relevant understanding of the liturgy. When the liturgy is understood not primarily as some historical structure but as a living event in the Church, it will lead to a desire for a study of liturgy that will show more regard for the actual meaning of the liturgy. This points to an extension of the purpose of the study of liturgy in three directions, which can be described as "methodical", "pastoral" and "theological".

3. As far back as 1841 A. Graf made a critical survey of the then current liturgical textbooks and came to the conclusion that "insofar as the study of liturgy is concerned, we have numerous and sound preliminary studies for a history of the Catholic

---

[8] A. Stuiber, "Liturgik," in *Lexikon für Theologie und Kirche* VI (²1961), p. 1095. Similarly, M. Righetti, *Manuale di Storia Liturgica* I (Milan, ³1964), p. 56.

[9] A. Stuiber, *loc. cit.* L. Fendt, *Einführung in die Liturgiewissenschaft* (Berlin, 1958), p. 1, reduces the (Evangelical) study of liturgy to the historical and exegetical treatment of the liturgical texts as "part of history of the Church or of dogma" as distinct from the purely practical approach.

[10] P. Oppenheim, *op. cit.*, p. xiii: "Historiam liturgiae potius tradunt quam ipsam liturgiam"; C. Callewaert, *op. cit.*, p. 174; A. G. Martimort, *L'Eglise en Prière* (Tournai, ³1965), p. 13; W. J. O'Shea, "Liturgiology," in *New Catholic Encyclopedia* VIII (New York, 1967), p. 920.

liturgy. There is also a rich literature which is purely concerned with practical matters and aims at providing a direct means for the correct and dignified execution of the existing liturgy. But up until now we do not yet have a science of Catholic liturgy, a proper study of liturgy as such".[11] In his *Kritische Darstellung des gegenwärtigen Zustandes der Praktischen Theologie* he then asks: "Have we today one book which is not merely an empirical collection of existing data, which goes beyond an explanation of and an improvement upon the partial and inadequate study with the help of history and some liturgical principles? Have we really got a systematic study of our Catholic liturgy?"

Exactly eighty years later R. Guardini, who probably did not know of Graf's work, made a new attempt. In 1921 he demanded a new approach and a new treatment of the study of liturgy which he called "the systematic study of liturgy" to distinguish it from the existing understanding of this discipline. It should provide an answer to the question: "What is the liturgy today and what does it mean?" The liturgy was not "merely something that lay buried in writings and monuments of the past, something like the cult of Mithras, but confronts us today as the genuine expression of life of genuine religious communities, and particularly as the religious practice of the Catholic Church".[12] In Guardini's eyes the object of this systematic study of the liturgy was "the Church as living, sacrificing, praying and dispensing the mysteries of grace in the actual performance of her worship and in the relevant obligatory expressions of this".[13] In this he was aware of not having started anything basically new. Both before and after him the treatment of the meaning of worship in the present has been repeatedly put forward as one of the tasks of the study of liturgy, and it was admitted that a mere

[11] A. Graf, *Kritische Darstellung des gegenwärtigen Zustandes der Praktischen Theologie* (Tübingen, 1841), p. 300.

[12] R. Guardini, "Ueber die systematische Methode in der Liturgiewissenschaft," in *Jahrbuch f. Liturgiewissenschaft* 1 (1921), p. 97. Similar suggestions were made by L. C. Mohlberg, *Nochmals Ziele und Aufgaben für das Studium des christlichen Kultes* (Rome, 1957), pp. 14f.

[13] R. Guardini, *op. cit.*, p. 104.

explanation of the origins of the existing liturgy was not enough for this.[14] But Guardini based his demand for a systematic study on new scientific theories and his proposals were without doubt the result of the repercussions of the movements for liturgical renewal on the study of the liturgy.

4. At about the same time we have an example of the idea that the historical approach to the study of liturgy should be complemented by a *pastoral* approach. Dealing with the constantly arising question whether the study of the liturgy (as of homiletics and catechetics) was a subdivision of pastoral theology, J. Seitz said in his *Handbook of Pastoral Theology* that these disciplines could no longer be dealt with in pastoral theology. He only wished to take those elements of the three disciplines which were necessary for the explanation of pastoral problems. While the new autonomous study of liturgy was mainly historical and exegetical, he said, the practical pastoral aspect could not be neglected there. Pastoral theology therefore had to show how the priest must fulfill his task in worship and the administration of the sacraments in order to dispense the graces contained therein to the people. This section of pastoral theology he calls "the pastoral study of liturgy".[15] Apart from the question whether the pastoral study of liturgy can be limited to the function of the priest and the dispensation of the means of grace, Seitz's view is worth mentioning because his expression "pastoral study of liturgy" or "pastoral liturgy" came into widespread use in various roundabout ways.

Athanasius Wintersig, of the Abbey of Maria Laach, used this expression, and in his essay on "Pastoralliturgik" he developed a

[14] In spite of a greater emphasis on the historical aspect, cf. P. de Puniet, "La Méthode en matière de Liturgie," in *Cours et Conférences des Semaines Liturgiques* 2 (1914), pp. 41-70; L. Eisenhofer, "Liturgie," in *Kirchliches Handlexikon* II (Freiburg, 1912), p. 684.

[15] J. E. von Pruner, *Lehrbuch der Pastoraltheologie* I ed. by J. Seitz, (Paderborn, ³1920), p. 16. The editions edited by Pruner (1900 and 1904) do not yet have this expression, but the combination of the words occurs in Latin literature: P. Rigler, *Pastoralis liturgica seu intelligentia et regula ministerii liturgici* (Bozen, ²1864).

program for the study of a pastoral treatment of the liturgy which should accompany the historical and methodical treatment. Wintersig started from the premise that "the liturgy was the continuation of Christ's life as the high priest in the Church and that this was the true center of the religious life of the community of the faithful".[16] For that reason there should be a scientific discipline of this within theology. This "science of the liturgical life of the community should investigate and show whether and how the liturgical and priestly life of the community can be built up in the most varied conditions of place, person and culture".[17] Of a pastoral liturgy, whose outline he sketched in detail, Wintersig expected "that every liturgical function should have its organic place underneath, above and on every side of the religious life of the community, and all this in the context of the whole supernatural and natural existence of the community".[18] This makes it clear that he by no means considers the liturgy as the only task of the Church's activity; he in no way looks on pastoral liturgy as a substitute for pastoral theology. His essay is a first attempt to tackle the problems arising from the interrelation of liturgy and general pastoral care on the basis of a new understanding of the liturgy. It is true that such a scientific pastoral liturgy has never been worked out comprehensively,[19] yet Wintersig's pastoral liturgy showed its influence when in 1943 in France an institute for "liturgy and pastoral care" was set up and had to be given a name. It was called Centre Pastorale Liturgique (CPL), and this was for the French language "a new and unaccustomed combination of words".[20]

[16] A. Wintersig, "Pastoralliturgik," in *Jahrbuch f. Liturgiewissenschaft* 4 (1924), p. 166.

[17] Wintersig, *loc. cit.*, p. 158.

[18] Wintersig, *loc. cit.*, p. 160. Over against Guardini, Wintersig (*loc. cit.*, p. 165) maintains that the pastoral study of liturgy is not the mere application of the systematic study of liturgy since it also provides new knowledge based on new principles.

[19] Wintersig found support in R. Stapper, *Katholische Liturgik* (Münster, [6]1931), p. 2; F. Schubert, "Neubau der Liturgik?" in *Theologie und Glaube* 19 (1927), pp. 250-54.

[20] C. Rauch, "Die Liturgische Bewegung in Frankreich von 1943-53," in *Liturgisches Jahrbuch* 4 (1954), p. 27.

Although Wintersig's concept always envisaged a scientific discipline—he never spoke of a "pastoral liturgy"—and the founders of CPL were only concerned with one branch out of the many that constitute the whole pastoral work,[21] inaccurate translations of the name of the French center created the inappropriate term "pastoral liturgy" (*liturgia pastoralis*).[22] Since "liturgy" means worship itself, the addition of the word "pastoral" is superfluous: there is no such thing as a "pastoral Mass" or a "pastoral baptism" alongside of the celebration of Mass or baptism. On the other hand, those who wanted to emphasize the "pastoral" aspect of the liturgy wanted to express a necessary aspect of the treatment of, e.g., Mass and baptism, which not merely dealt with the history of the rites or their meaning in a systematic study of the liturgy, but also with their place and execution within the whole context of the Church's activity.

5. The view of liturgy as the central act of the Church, as the first and necessary source of the Christian spirit, as an event which glorifies God and sanctifies man, led to the demand for a

[21] P. Duployé, "Le Centre de Pastorale liturgique," in *Etudes de Pastorale Liturgique* (Paris, 1944), pp. 81-93; A. M. Roguet, "La pastorale liturgique oeuvre d'éducation," in *Questions Lit. et Par.* 36 (1955), p. 18; C. Morin, "Pour un mouvement liturgique pastoral," in *La Clarté-Dieu* 13 (Lyons, 1944), pp. 5-9; A. G. Martimort, "Dix ans de Pastorale liturgique en France," in *Maison-Dieu* 40 (1955), pp. 170-76. A. M. Roguet's definition of "pastoral" in "La pastorale liturgique," in *L'Eglise en Prière* (Tournai, ³1965), pp. 237f., as determining the meaning of pastoral liturgy, was rightly opposed by C. Floristan Samanes, *Teologia de la Accion Pastoral* (Madrid, 1968), pp. 383f. and M. Löhrer, "Die Feier des Mysteriums der Kirche (Kulttheologie und Liturgie der Kirche)," in *Handbuch der Pastoraltheologie* I (Freiburg, 1964), p. 292. For the objects of a pastoral liturgy, see also Vagaggini, *op. cit.*, pp. 402-18. That, as Vagaggini maintains on p. 412, the concept of "pastoral liturgy" or better "liturgical pastoral theology" only arose after the movements for renewal since World War II is not correct.

[22] Pastoral liturgy in Parsch, *Volksliturgie* (Klosterneuburg, ²1950), in the Preface. The *Ephemerides Liturgicae* 67 (1953), p. 415, introduced the heading "Liturgia Pastoralis" for the first time in its annual Index. In an address Pope Pius XII spoke of those "who were present at the international congress on pastoral liturgy" (*AAS* 48, 1956), p. 711. See also the reports of this Congress in various languages with the expressions: "pastoral liturgy" (Collegeville, 1957), "liturgia pastoral" (Toledo, 1957), and "liturgia pastorale" (Genoa, 1957).

broadening of the liturgical themes from a theological point of view. In 1912 L. Beauduin tried to work out the place of the liturgy in the total structure of salvation history.[23] Several official pronouncements on liturgical training, particularly of the clergy, pointed out theological aspects which had to be taken into consideration.[24] C. Vagaggini, who contributed much of the material, demanded a theological study of the liturgy which would show the place which liturgy should have in the general dispensation of salvation according to revelation and which would deal with the elements of the liturgy from a theological point of view.[25] It was repeatedly pointed out that the Church's worship needs to be studied by other theological disciplines as well and could not be left to the study of liturgy alone.[26]

A brief survey of the various theories revealed the divergent opinions already current with regard to the tasks and aims of the study of liturgy. In spite of this divergence, we already see there —apart from such exceptions to be mentioned later on—a remarkable agreement on two points:

First of all, the study of liturgy was seen above all as material for the training and formation of the priest. Even where the liturgy was not seen as merely the concern of the clergy but more comprehensively as the action of all the members of the Church, the study of liturgy aimed mainly at the clergy, at providing the priest with the right understanding and discharge of the liturgical function and at enabling him to educate the laity to the same level.

Second, this study of the liturgy—regardless of whether it emphasized the rubrics, the history, the method, the pastoral aspect

[23] L. Beauduin, "Essai de nauel fondamental de Liturgie," in *Questions liturgiques* 3 (1912/13), pp. 56-66.

[24] Cf. H. B. Meyer, "Liturgie als Hauptfach," in *Zeitschr. f. Kath. Theol.* 88 (1966), pp. 315-35.

[25] In his work mentioned in n. 1. One should also take note of the evangelical approach in P. Brunner, "Zur Lehre von Gottesdienst der im Namen Jesu versammelten Gemeinde," in *Leiturgia* I (Kassel, 1954), pp. 83-364.

[26] Cf. H. B. Meyer, " 'Liturgische Theologie' oder 'Theologie des Gottesdienstes'," in *Zeitschr. f. Kath. Theol.* 86 (1964), pp. 327-31. See also M. Löhrer, *op. cit.*, pp. 290-307.

or the theological aspects—dealt almost exclusively either with earlier and for a large part "dead" liturgies or with the liturgy prevailing at the time, as laid down by the authorities in the liturgical books or other ecclesiastical documents in the shape of texts, notes or regulations for the organization of worship and related questions.

We have to ask ourselves, however, whether such a view of the tasks of the study of liturgy is still adequate today.

The Study of Liturgy: More than a Matter of Professional Training

I have no intention of denying the urgent need for a liturgical training—whatever this means in detail —of theological students, whether clerical or lay, particularly if the lay students are going to take on various ecclesiastical functions. No long argument, however, is necessary to prove that the task of theology in the Church stretches well beyond the training for an ecclesiastical function as the exclusive or main purpose. It would therefore be senseless to look for the aims of a theological discipline in the timetable of a syllabus in some ecclesiastical training center. Theology existed long before there was any special ecclesiastical training. It is rather an essential function of the Church to think methodically and scientifically about the Word and saving activity of God, to unfold it and to interpret it according to the changes in the historical situation of the faithful. Here the Church herself and her work are not merely an object of theological analysis in the unchanging structure of her nature; also needed is theological reflection about what she achieves in her life insofar as this implies constant changes in the concrete situations of the time. K. Rahner saw here the real task of "practical theology" which is more than a pastoral theology in the strict sense, too exclusively concerned with the duties of a "pastor". This "practical theology" must treat of "the actual self-fulfilment of the Church insofar as this can be known through a scientific reflection on the essence of the Church and through a theological analysis of the present situation, both critical (what is actually happening) and normative (what should happen)".[27] Since worship belongs to the elementary, permanent and irreplaceable life-tasks of the Church, it must also be treated in this way by theology. The task of the study of liturgy is then to reflect theologically on worship in the Church, as it actually takes place in the Church and as it ought to be according to the knowledge we derive from the lasting structure of the Church and the theological analysis of the contemporary historical situation of the Church.[28]

The Liturgy as the Constantly New Object of Liturgical Study

And so, our position is already clear with regard to the further question which links up with the historical survey of the various opinions about the aim of the study of liturgy. It is not enough for a study of liturgy to limit itself to the study of earlier or present liturgies. It is its duty toward the Church to reflect upon other possible forms of liturgy and to develop both principles and concrete applications to meet the demands of a relevant act of worship in the contemporary situation of the Church. K. Rahner points to this aim of the study of liturgy when he writes: "The present study of liturgy no longer has as its prime object the history and evaluation of the existing liturgy but theological reflection on a liturgy which has still to be created." [29] One may well wonder, though, whether the study of liturgy has already achieved this in actual fact, and whether we should not see in Rahner's words an exhortation rather than a statement of fact.

It is hardly surprising that the object of the study of liturgy as presented here has not yet found expression in the liturgical pub-

[27] K. Rahner, "Grundlegung der Pastoraltheologie als praktischer Theologie," in Handbuch der Pastoraltheologie I (Freiburg, 1964), pp. 117f.

[28] In accordance with the ideas laid down in the Handbuch der Pastoral theologie, M. Löhrer has made some initial attempts at drafting such a program (op. cit., I, pp. 287-323), the execution of which seem to fall behind with the suggestion on p. 292, probably because of limitation of space and lack of required theological analyses.

[29] K. Rahner, "Die Praktische Theologie im Ganzen der Theologischen Disziplinen," in Die Praktische Theologie zwischen Wissenschaft und Praxis (Munich, 1968), pp. 62f.

lications during the last decades. As long as the liturgy was seen as fixed, ready-made and practically unalterable, and its lack of relevance with regard to the actual situations and needs of the Church was upheld and defended, there was neither room nor desire for a theological discipline which should deal with a "liturgia condenda" (a liturgy still to be created—K. Rahner). This observation also explains partly why the study of liturgy helped indeed to indirectly prepare the reform of the liturgy by its historical research but in the beginning lagged behind the movements for renewal and played no leading part in these movements. There was only a small group of liturgical scholars who saw "in the zeal for liturgical reform a passing of the Spirit through his Church" (*Constitution on the Sacred Liturgy*, n. 43). This may, however, also partly be due to the fact that scientific reflection by nature always begins with a certain hesitation.

In the *Constitution on the Sacred Liturgy* we have a document with a concept of the liturgy which does not just allow these aims of a critical and normative study of liturgy but demands them. The pronouncements contained in that text on the nature of the liturgy and its relevance for the Church's life do not mean to be the last word on this subject, but rather indicate certain directives for further development. Since the conciliar conclusions about reform do not wish to replace "the old liturgy" by a "new", equally rigid liturgy but rather lead to an "open" liturgy (which is not the same as an "arbitrary" one), the search for the best way in which the Church can realize herself in her acts of worship remains a permanent object of the state of liturgy. When the Constitution says that one of the aims is "to adapt more suitably to the needs of our own times those institutions which are subject to change" (n. 1; see also nn. 21, 23, 62, 88), it clearly expresses the dynamic elements in the Council's idea of the liturgy. The "needs of our time" can always be better understood and therefore demand other solutions; the needs of the next generation can again lead to other consequences for the way worship should operate and be fitted into the overall activity of the

Church. The basic principle of the Constitution may be summarized as applying the principle of a Church which is constantly in a state of reform (*ecclesia semper reformanda*) to the liturgy which is also constantly in a state of reform (*liturgia semper reformanda*). And the implied renewal must not be understood as limited to eliminating possible abuses but as that always necessary renewal of a Church endowed with all the potential that must lead to fullness and pluriformity. It is a mistake to think that the liturgical reform is simply an occasional and limited enterprise which will "fix" the liturgy again so that it becomes once again a "ready-made liturgy" for another long period. The task of the new study of liturgy, as described above, is therefore not a passing occupation but a permanent obligation.

Insofar as the study of liturgy is a subject that appears on the syllabus of a seminary, the above-mentioned aims do not strike one as primary. By the same token discussions about whether and how far such a study should be a part of a "practical theology" or have a relative autonomy also strike one as of secondary importance. The former, occasionally rather fierce emphasis on its autonomy with regard to pastoral theology was provoked by the narrow concept of pastoral theology which prevailed for a long time. A critical and normative study of liturgy will in any case have to make extensive use of the theological analyses of the present condition of the Church, made in the "practical theology" of which Rahner spoke. But it will also have to deal with issues which a practical theology will barely touch upon; it will have to offer concrete applications which practical theology as such cannot provide. There is therefore no need to suspect or fear that the approach to the study of liturgy as set out here will in the end lead to the disappearance of this study in pastoral theology.

It seems to me not enough, and even fatal, for the study of liturgy if the above-mentioned aims of this study were simply seen as *one of the many possible* (perhaps wholly desirable) tasks of this study, side by side with a juridical, historical, systematic, pastoral or theological study of liturgy. I rather mean that insofar as these aspects do not belong in actual fact to the history of the Church or of dogma or to a practical training course, these aspects have their essential place in a critical and normative study of liturgy and can only be properly integrated in this approach to the science of liturgy. A theological study "of the worshiping assemblies in the name of Jesus", their place and achievement within the overall fulfillment of the Church in her contemporary condition (and also in the future) might without doubt save it from that narrow approach from which so many studies of liturgical material suffered in the past. With these new aims we may perhaps begin to realize that, for all the scientific prowess shown in the earlier studies, theology, creative power, imagination and inspiration do not exclude each other but belong together.

It is obvious that the study of liturgy as understood in this article must make far more use of the data provided by the anthropological sciences than in the past. And here I do not mean that an already existing liturgy should be confronted with the psychology of religion, sociology, psychology in depth and social psychology, linguistic sciences and music. It is rather a case of using these sciences in the planning of and experimenting with the liturgy. "For, only when we know the human conditions of the Christian of today . . . can we answer the question of *what shape* the liturgy should take *today*".[30] A "handbook for the study of liturgy" which would quote the early medieval sacramentaries more often than contemporary anthropological studies would in the future no longer be justified in claiming to be such a "handbook".

As to the demarcation of the object of this new study of liturgy, one should be aware of the fact that this is one of the first tasks of such a study. It is obviously not a matter of how the word "liturgy" is used. Nevertheless, the widely current assignment of specific acts of worship to the categories of worship used in the Constitution (n. 13)—namely, "liturgy", "sacred practices of local Churches" (*sacra particularium Ecclesiarum exer-*

[30] K. Rahner, *op. cit.*, p. 63.

citia) and "pious exercises" (*pia exercitia*)—seems rather arbitrary. It would mean, for instance, that when a priest reads his breviary in a railway compartment, that is "liturgy", while a public Corpus Christi procession with the bishop, many clergy and laity, is not "liturgy" but "only" a "sacred practice" of a local Church. In fact, practically the whole scope of "public ecclesiastical worship", including liturgical assemblies for the celebration of the sacraments, constitutes the subject matter of the critical and normative study of the liturgy.[31] And it is of no consequence whether or not such acts of worship can be found in liturgical books that are approved by Rome, the bishops or nobody at all, or merely appear on television.

The Critical and Normative Study of Liturgy and Official Authority

One may object to such a view of the aims of the study of liturgy that it lays claim to powers to which it is not entitled, but which belong to the ecclesiastical authorities. Did the Constitution not lay down in so many words that "the regulation of the sacred liturgy depends solely on the authority of the Church" (n. 22)?

It seems to me that our idea of a critical and normative study of liturgy does not contradict this statement of the Council. We should, first of all, remember that the new liturgical regulations are, according to the indications contained in the Constitution, largely meant as a kind of framework. A bishops' conference or the actual religious assembly can legitimately choose among the proffered possibilities according to circumstances and the situation. To try to establish some criteria as a guide for such a choice is therefore a task which in no way interferes with the rights of the authorities.

But our view of the object of this study goes beyond that, and

---

[31] The separate treatment of liturgy and sacraments in the *Handbuch der Pastoraltheologie* I, p. 217 (see n. 27) is due to a too narrow understanding of the sacrament. Cf. M. Löhrer, *op. cit.*, I, pp. 289 and 293.

we expect it to provide not only principles but also concrete applications to help in creating a liturgy as it ought to be. On this point it seems to us that the relation between the regulating authority and the study of liturgy should follow the same lines as those that govern these relations in other theological disciplines. Theology neither can be, nor means to be, a substitute for the magisterium or practical official guidance, but respects these functions. Like the other disciplines the study of liturgy offers the results of its work but leaves the decision about their application to others. But this does not mean either that such a study then becomes superfluous, because with regard to the practical realization it remains a "conditional" science. When canonists make suggestions about the feasibility of the abolition of certain impediments of marriage or the introduction of new ones, or when practical theology puts out proposals for a better demarcation of dioceses, all this is also "conditional". The possibility of introducing data of the study of liturgy into practice in some minor way without looking at the decisions of authority is no reason to abandon this normative research or to turn it into a kind of secret science. Unsatisfactory regulations of liturgical matters by official ecclesiastical authorities remain binding, but remain nevertheless unsatisfactory; to see them as such is not contempt of court. "The theologian's willingness to listen does not indeed lead to a kind of obedience where all his scientifically established facts, his research and his conclusions simply aim at conformity with authority." [32] That the critical function of such a study of liturgy, like all its other functions, should take place in the spirit of a kind of "moral code" of such a study would appear obvious: "A scientific treatment of the liturgy . . . which refuses to be of service, at least indirectly, to the loving performance of the liturgy must be considered not only futile but even pernicious." [33]

[32] M. D. Chenu, "Die Theologie als kirchliche Wissenschaft," in *Concilium* 3 (1967), p. 47.

[33] B. Fischer, *Tamquam machina quaedam* . . . ("Ein Wort Augustins zum Ethos der Liturgiewissenschaft," in *Miscellanea Liturgica* II (Rome, 1967), p. 89.

For the rest, as A. Graf pointed out long ago, the decisions of ecclesiastical authorities also need the guidance of science.[34] Referring to Graf, a handbook of Catholic liturgy observed in 1912: "As a positive and theological discipline, the study of liturgy cannot do without the ecclesiastical authority, but the bearer of this ecclesiastical authority should also be willing to be interested in this study and assimilate and apply the data it provides." [35]

The Teaching of Liturgy in Ecclesiastical Training Centers

In conclusion I want to mention one more point—namely, the study of liturgy as a teaching subject. It should by now be obvious that this study as described above cannot be simply identified with the courses in theology which take place in training centers for service in the Church and deal with liturgical themes. Insofar as the clergy are concerned, the Constitution has laid down a number of important directives with which I cannot deal here. The study of liturgy as envisaged in that conciliar document aims at the training of the clergy. It would be wrong to see there an exhaustive description of the tasks implied in the study of liturgy. There is also an "Instruction on the Liturgical Formation of the Clergy", published by the Congregation for Seminaries and Universities in 1965, which contributes nothing to the organization of a critical and normative study of liturgy, apart from the obvious flaws in this Instruction which on many points takes no notice of the decisions reached by the Council (which explains why it has not been promulgated in the official organ of the Holy See, in spite of its being confirmed by the pope in advance).[36]

Although the immediate purpose of instructions about the liturgy in ecclesiastical institutions at various levels (priests, pastoral helpers, sacristans, organists and choirmasters) is bound to differ from that of the study of liturgy as such, it should not

[34] A. Graf, op. cit., pp. 188-90.

[35] V. Thalhofer and L. Eisenhofer, op. cit., I, p. 62.

[36] S. C. Seminariis et Studiorum Universitatibus, Instructio de sacrorum alumnorum liturgica institutione (Rome, 1965). A later edition called it an "Excerptum e Commentario 'Seminarium' n. 1., A.D. 1966."

overlook relevant problems that have emerged in this study of liturgy. The aim of such instructions is to create full cooperation, in the widest sense of the word, in the Church's liturgy, and this cannot be limited to telling people how to take part in and conduct a religious assembly. Such teaching should educate those who are particularly responsible for the religious service to liturgical adulthood with due respect for the official regulations. It is here that such teaching would be greatly assisted by close contact with those who deal professionally with this critical and normative study of liturgy.

Helmut Hucke/*Neu Isenburg, West Germany*

Jazz and Folk Music in the Liturgy

For some time church musicians, liturgists and the general public have been following various attempts to introduce everyday music genres into the liturgy. There has been much talk about playing folk music, jazz, and rhythm and blues in church. Young people's Masses and new religious songs have come into vogue.

This article is a preliminary report on the whole phenomenon —how far it has spread and where it stands today. To compile this report, we sent out a questionnaire to various people and supplemented their replies with information gained from reading and from personal contacts around the world.

The following people replied to our questionnaire more or less completely and provided us with a great deal of information: Anthony Newman, The Entrance, N.S.W., Australia; José Weber, Rio de Janeiro, Brazil; Johannes Aengenvoort, Essen, Germany; Peter Morison, London, England; Paul Zurfluh, Paris, France; Stephen Somerville, Toronto, Canada; Saburo Takata, Tokyo, Japan; Marijan Smolik, Ljubljana, Yugoslavia; Alberto Taulé Viñas, Barcelona, Spain.

I
BASIC MUSICAL CATEGORIES AND CONCEPTS

Let us first take a look at some of the basic concepts and musical genres that are involved in these new experiments and in discussions about them.

The Negro Spiritual

This is a category of folk music that developed among American negroes in the southern states. It has found widespread appeal since the end of slavery, particularly through its tieup with jazz which is partially rooted in the spiritual.

This development has taken two forms: choral arrangements for several voices, sung primarily by student ensembles, and solo arrangements with instrumental accompaniment, designed mainly for records and personal appearances. In recent years these spirituals have been translated from English into other languages. The melodies have also been incorporated into song books.

Jazz

Jazz arose at the end of the 19th century among American negroes in the south. It fused elements of Afro-American folk music (especially the spiritual), western popular music, marching music and other strains. World War I brought jazz to Europe. Since then, with the help of radio, records and the other mass media, it has spread all over the world. The development of jazz has seen the rise of many divergent and differing styles.

In jazz a given melody is played improvisationally by the individual members of the combo or band, in accordance with some basic formal rules. The rhythm section maintains a steady underlying *beat*. Over against this beat, the melody section plays assymetrical phrases with free accentuation (the *offbeat*), so that the rhythms overlap (*swing*). Minor and major thirds and sevenths are treated neutrally (*blue notes*), and there are specific types of intonation and rhythmic phrasing.

The element of improvisation is one of the characteristic features of jazz, so that jazz defies notation. The same piece is never played exactly the same, even by one and the same band.

By its very nature, jazz playing is the province of specialists and dedicated enthusiasts. Not everything that is labeled jazz in popular parlance is authentic jazz, but jazz has exerted enormous influence on the music of the mass media. Some of its characteristic traits and playing styles have become familiar elements in popular music, helping to shape "the sound".

Other musicians and composers have been stimulated by the techniques of jazz on occasion (e.g., Igor Stravinsky, Darius Milhaud, Ernst Krenek, Rolf Liebermann). In his recent compositions, Heinz Werner Zimmermann, the director of the Protestant school of church music in Berlin, has come to terms with jazz.[1] By the same token, some jazz musicians have concerned themselves with other forms of musical composition, and in recent years they have shown a serious interest in church music. Most of the resultant compositions are quite difficult and demanding to perform.

The Chanson

This is a type of song composed of verses, which treats some romantic, sentimental or satiric theme. Of French vintage, it has been a popular genre from the Middle Ages to the present day. Since the middle of the 19th century, it has become a favorite genre of the Parisian cabaret singer (the *chansonnier*), who often composes his own lyrics and intersperses the melody with rapidly spoken patter (e.g., Edith Piaf, Charles Aznavour).

[1] "Die Möglichkeiten und Grenzen des Jazz innerhalb der Musiksprache der Gegenwart": lecture at the first convention of German church musicians, Berlin 1959. *Musica sacra in unserer Zeit* (Berlin, 1960), pp. 49-67. Compositions (on records): "Das Vater Unser", "Lobet ihr Knechte, des Herren", "Uns ist ein Kind geboren" (Cantate 643 235); "Psalmkonzert" (Cantate 640 229); Vesper—Motets—Christmas song (Cantate 658 217).

Music for the Masses

The development of the mass media, particularly radio and records, has brought about a whole new set of conditions for the production, reproduction and marketing of music. People no longer have to sing or play music themselves or go to a concert. There are no longer any social barriers preventing the individual from enjoying the sound of music. A whole new music public has come into being, and an entirely new set of listening habits has taken shape.

With the push of a button, a person can be surrounded with music whenever and wherever he wants. It can be almost any type of music, but much of it is a new brand of music produced for a mass market. It is not so much a musical composition as an arrangement of sounds. You may be able to hum the melody, but you can only get the original on a record. The music utilizes current techniques and effects, following the dance craze of the day and the latest jazz styles.

The lyrics deal with certain basic themes: unrequited love, homesickness, loneliness, etc. The listener need not listen carefully, much less pay attention to the words. This music is meant simply to serve as background noise. In recent years, many business establishments (e.g., restaurants and coffee houses) have sought to exploit the subliminal effects of this music, installing sound systems and speakers with great care for placement and noise level.

The Hit Tune

This is a piece of music that proves to be very popular with the public and sells well. The music industry also applies the label to new tunes which it hopes will sell well. Many types of music may make it: popular music, marches, chansons, opera arias, or classical pieces. The main gauge of success is the number of records sold, but the "charts" also take into account how often it is played in juke boxes, on disk jockey shows, and in other renditions.

Folk Songs and Folk Music

A wave of interest in folk music, originating in the United States, has gradually spread all over the world. In many parts of the world, in fact, the English words "folk song" and "folk music" have replaced or overshadowed the vernacular equivalents. They refer to traditional pieces of folk music that are taken out of their original setting and adapted to the modern audience.

The tunes may be those of one's own people or those of another land. They can be authentic or newly created, vocal or instrumental, ballad, spiritual or chanson. Here, too, the arrangement, the execution and "the sound" play a major role. The melody and the notation are merely the raw materials for the finished product.

Folk music has its stars also. But one can also make his own folk music, usually to the accompaniment of a guitar. The guitar has become the primary source for the "sound" of folk music, and its popularity has never been so great or so widespread.

II
NEW RELIGIOUS SONGS AND HYMNS

Beginnings

Even in the 19th century, church hymns had already adopted the style of secular songs, imitating patriotic songs and sentimental mood music. Some of these hymns are still used in the Catholic Church. The rise of the mass music industry, however, created a whole new situation insofar as this process was concerned.

The negro spiritual was included in the repertory of the music industry from the very beginning. Then, inspired by the rousing songs of the old revival meetings, Americans began to produce and market new religious songs through the new mass industry. In 1940 singer Roy Acuff brought out the song *Radio Station*

Saved, which became a hit in the United States and had great success elsewhere.[2]

In the mid 1950s new religious songs created a stir in Europe also. In 1956 the Pro Civitate Cristiana Institute in Italy invited songwriters and composers to create new religious songs, and it organized a festival in Assisi. In early 1957 the German record industry brought out German renditions of two American religious songs, performed by two top entertainers.[3] Because of adverse reactions from ecclesiastical authorities, however, the records were not kept on the air, and the record industry dropped the experiment.

Aimé Duval, S.J.

Apart from the efforts to enlist the music industry and its stars in the service of Christian proclamation, we must note the efforts of priests, teachers and church-sponsored youth organizations to find a form of musical expression that would be both modern and in line with the national spirit. One of the first to make serious efforts in this direction was Father Aimé Duval, S.J.[4] in France.

[2] Walter Haas, *Das Schlagerbuch* (Munich, 1957), p. 72.

[3] "Es war im Anfang" (In the Beginning) and "Wer" (He): Electrola 17-8650; the latter song is also recorded on Decca 18 325. The radio director for the Evangelical Church in Germany explained his position thus: "We indeed realize that songs with religious lyrics have gone over well in America and Italy. In America, of course, the negro spiritual has stimulated a whole movement in music, and its reverberations can even be felt by us here in Germany. Moreover, the tradition of popular religious songs is deeply rooted in America and Italy, and we find similar efforts among the Methodists and the Salvation Army. Interestingly enough, all such experiments have met with rejection in Germany. . . . I think that we are particularly concerned to know whether there is a proper correspondence between the content of a song and its musical form. Take "He", for example. It is unabashed emotionalism, leading to the conclusion that God is the source of all these emotional feelings. . . . I can only regard it as a return to sentimentalism in religion. Speaking on behalf of the Evangelical Church in Germany, I can only say that not only would we not support such a production but we would actually deplore it": Haas, *Das Schlagerbuch*, p. 74.

[4] Records by Studio SM, Paris; lyrics and melodies by Editions de l'Ept, Paris.

He was soon followed by Father Auguste M. Cocagnac, O.P.,[5] Marie Claire Pichaud and Soeur Sourire. They utilized a traditional French genre, the chanson, and played their own songs in their own individual styles.

Since 1957, religious chansons have attained widespread popularity in France and elsewhere. The main channel of distribution has been records; these records usually contain the original French version even when they are distributed in a foreign market. This manner of distribution tells us something about the close relationship between text and interpretation in this music. It also suggests that students in high school and college are the most enthusiastic devotees of these songs among young people.

In Italy, Italian translations of the original text are recommended for "catechetical reflection".

Tutzing Academy

Another initiative in this area came from a Protestant school in Germany. In 1961, Tutzing Academy sponsored a contest for new religious songs, and three more contests have been held since then.[6] Some of the prize winners have been Martin G.

[5] Records by Disques Lumen, Paris; lyrics and melodies, Editions du Cerf, Paris.

[6] Cf. *Warum neue religiöse Lieder?* edited by Günter Hegele (Regensburg, 1964). Records: "Danke"/ "Antwort auf alle Fragen" (the Botho-Lucas Choir, Electrola E 22073); "Danke"/ "Verlorener Weg"/ "Weihnachtslied"/ "Christ ist erstanden" (St. Matthew's Choir, Munich, Cantate 643 306); "Weil du ja zu mir sagst"/ "Ein Schiff, das sich Gemeinde nennt"/ "Der Weg der Barmherzigkeit"/ "Funde am Weg"/ "Lasst uns spüren"/ "Gott meint es gut mit dir"/ "Im Garten von Gethsemane"/ "Ich zieh meiner dunklen Strasse"/ "Der Teufel"/ "Wehr dich nicht"/ "Gott ist der Herr" (the Botho-Lucas Choir, Kenneth Spencer, Ralf Bendix, Electrola E 83 512); "Ich zieh meiner dunklen Strasse"/ "Funde am Weg" (the Botho-Lucas Choir, Electrola E 22 534); "Im Garten von Gethsemane"/ "Lasst us spüren" (Kenneth Spencer, Electrola 22 535); "Gott meint es gut mit dir"/ "Wehr dich nicht" (the Botho-Lucas Choir, Electrola E 22 536); "Der Teufel"/ "Strasse des Lebens" (Ralf Bendix Electrola E 22 537); "Weil du ja zu mir sagst"/ "Weg der Barmherzigkeit" (Ralf Bendix Electrola 22 538); "Gott ist der Herr"/ "Ein Schiff, das sich Gemeinde nennt"

Schneider, Oskar G. Blau, Bernard Schulé, Christine Heuser and Friedrich Walz. The arrangements and finished recordings are usually the work of professionals.

On the Catholic side in Germany, Fathers Fleury, Riedel and Ballestrem have followed the lead of Father Aimé Duval. The overall picture in Germany is quite complex because a wide variety of influences has been at work (e.g., the spiritual, the chanson, mod dances, older hymns). The new experiments have not been restricted to West Germany. Dietrich Mendt, a Protestant pastor in East Germany, has written quite a few "new songs"; from all reports it seems that young people in East Germany are just as interested as their counterparts in West Germany.

The results of our questionnaire indicate that the main stimuli in this area have been the negro spiritual and other American genres, the French chanson, and German songs.

III

New Songs in the Liturgy

In Catholic circles at least, the new songs were not originally composed for the liturgy or other church services. But it was not much of a jump to introduce suitable songs into the liturgy and to adopt the new style of song for liturgical celebrations.

(Botho-Lucas Choir, Electrola E 22 539); Choräle, Songs und Neue Lieder: Neue geistliche Lieder vom Evangelischen Kirchentag (Philips P 48 049 L); "Weil du ja zu mir sagst"/ "Bleibe bei uns, Herr"/ "Lass uns spüren" (Musica Nova Choir, Christiana CGS 12 002); "Gott meint es gut mit dir"/ "Kennst du den Vater Abraham"/ "Selig sind die geistlich Armen"/ "Du bist bei mir" (Christiana CGS 12 003); "Der Teufel"/ "Rahab, ein Freudenmädchen"/ "Da stimmt das nicht"/ "Das Gesetz von Sinai" (Christiana CGS 12 004). Music books: Danke. Songs from the first music contest of Tutzing Academy (Bosse pub., Regensburg); Weil du ja zu mir sagst. Songs from the second music contest of Tutzing Academy (Bosse pub., Regensburg); Gott ist da. Songs from the third music contest of Tutzing Academy (Bosse, Regensburg); Wenn Gott es will. Songs from the fourth music contest of Tutzing Academy (Bosse, Regensburg).

Liturgical Reform and the Music of the People

Into this situation was injected the liturgical reform of Vatican Council II. Singing was to be an integral part of the liturgy. The people were to sing, and to sing in their own language. All over the world, people were suddenly faced with the task of providing liturgical songs in their own language.

The existing situation varied from country to country. Only a few areas—the German-speaking world in particular—had a living tradition where church music was tied up with the music of the people. In many places (France in particular), popular church music of this sort had come into vogue shortly before Vatican Council II convened. In large parts of the world, however, only a few devotional hymns were in use.

This deplorable state of affairs also applied to Gregorian chant. Despite all exhortations and efforts, its use was extremely limited. With the exception of a few areas (the German-speaking world in particular), choral sacred music had not been kept up even in cathedral churches. And even where church choirs still flourished and the people were accustomed to singing, the existing repertory was hardly adequate. New songs would have to be developed.

One might have expected composers of these new songs to pattern their pieces after Gregorian chant and traditional hymns. Many did this, to be sure, but it soon became evident that the style and structure of these prototypes would not do for the present task. Moreover, the *Constitution on the Sacred Liturgy* embodies a new appreciation of the liturgy and liturgical singing. Didn't *aggiornamento* call for a new, contemporary idiom in the liturgy?

Interestingly enough, the same questions were being raised in Protestant circles. Even though there was no movement toward overall liturgical reform, a jaundiced eye was being cast on existing hymnals. Young people were the most dissatisfied group, but they were not alone in their discontent.

The First Experiments

As early as 1952, a "Twentieth-Century Folk Mass" was celebrated under the direction of Geoffrey Beaumont. It utilized jazz
elements in the Introit and Credo. The Mass was picked up by
television and reproduced on records, and it had a wide impact.[7]

The earliest date given for such experiments in our questionnaire is 1963—Canada and Germany. (Unfortunately, we found
no correspondent for our questionnaire in the United States.)
Since that time, many independent initiatives have been undertaken in all parts of the world within a relatively short period of
time.

In Germany Johannes Acngenvoort regards 1964/1965 as
the "boom" period. In 1965 Brazil held its first convention on
folk music in the liturgy. As far as we know from our questionnaire, 1965 also saw the first official expression of opinion by a
territorial bishop—specifically, by the archbishop of Cologne.
1966 appears to have been the year for breakthroughs in many
lands.

The International Study Week on singing and liturgical renewal, which was held in Freiburg, Switzerland in the summer of
1965, did not take up the problem of new experiments. Nor was
it discussed directly by the Sacred Congregation of Rites when it
drew up *Musicam sacram* (published belatedly on March 5,
1967), even though press releases tried to tie it in with "jazz"
and "rock" Masses. It first appeared on the agenda of an international Catholic convention when the International Church
Music Congress (Consociatio Internationalis Musicae Sacrae)
convened in Milwaukee and Chicago in the summer of 1966.[8]

Developments around the World

UNITED STATES: Informed reports about this international
congress indicate that the American delegates attempted to bring
these experiments out into the open, and to discuss the value of

[7] Rochus Hagen, *Jazz in der Kirche?* (Stuttgart, 1967), p. 29.
[8] The proceedings of the Congress are not yet available.

folk and guitar Masses. A sharp division apparently arose between the American delegates, who saw these experiments as positive and necessary things, and the European delegates, who were against them.[9]

CANADA: Stephen Somerville reports that, as far as he can see, folk Masses have become quite common. Guitar accompaniment is so commonplace that they are often called "guitar Masses". Other instruments are also used on occasion: banjos, accordions, flutes, violins, drums, tambourines, pianos, saxophones, clavichords, percussion instruments and tape recorders. The spirit of Psalm 150 is alive once again.

Somerville's report suggests that guitar Masses are celebrated quite regularly in half of the parishes of the Toronto archdiocese. A major source for these experiments is a student organization in the University of Toronto, which has had an exceptionally dynamic priest-moderator since 1964. Most of the guitar Masses, it seems, are the result of collaboration between young priests and youth directors.

The new texts derive mainly from "the younger generation", but sometimes from priests and musicians. The musicians, however, are usually young vocalists and instrumentalists. Some of the music is composed by the group itself, and in certain areas they are responsible for most of it.[10]

AUSTRALIA: Anthony Newman reports that the use of folk music styles in church music is a very recent innovation. It began among Catholic student groups, spreading from liturgical services in schools to parish services for young people. Negro spirituals were sung at first, but they soon gave rise to original compositions. New texts are often composed for well-known

[9] See the following reports on the Congress: "Experimentation with New Music in the Liturgy Is Defended," in *The Catholic Messenger* (Sept. 8, 1966); "Congress of Lost Opportunities," in *America* (Sept. 24, 1966). Sample American experiments: *Mass for Young Americans* (Record and Book), F.E.L. Publications, Chicago; Joe Masters, Jazz Mass.

[10] Record: The Canticle of the Gift (Markle productions, M-15 001).

melodies. The results are usually second-rate, and these compositions are gradually being replaced by other songs. Much of the repertory derives from the United States.

Of the new songs composed in Australia itself, two basic styles can be distinguished. The first is based on that of Lucien Deiss and others in France. The second is a folk music style with guitar accompaniment.[11]

JAPAN: Saburo Takata reports that up to now there have been few initiatives to compose chansons and songs for the liturgy. The use of these genres in the liturgy is not yet an issue in the country. In Tokyo, however, one group of Japanese youth does sing jazz-type songs in Masses attended by Americans.

ENGLAND: Peter Morison reports that in recent years a large number of new religious songs have appeared. Many of them have been composed by nuns for instructional purposes. Now and then one hears about a liturgical service for some particular occasion or group, but there is no widespread interest as yet. In St. John's Seminary (Wonersh), attempts to compose liturgical texts in a folk music style have met with some success.

Such experiments are not widespread in the Anglican Church either. The "Twentieth Century Light Music Group" has brought out a series of new melodies for songs and psalms, but they have not written any new lyrics. The melodies are usually played at services for young people or at missions.[12]

GERMANY: Johannes Aengenvoort reports that records have done much to introduce the new religious songs to young people.

[11] Peter Kearney, "Songs Of Brotherhood" (J. Albert & Sons, Sidney); "Throw Open Your Hearts" by the Sisters of the Loreto Convent, Normanhurst, N.S.W. (Allan's Music, Ltd.); "People Of God", Mass hymns by Mother B. M. Moore of the Sacre Coeur Convent, Glen Iris, Victoria (J. Albert & Sons, Sidney).

[12] Published: Hymns, set by Malcolm Williamson (Weinberger); Anglican Mass, by Rev. Timothy Beaumont (Weinberger); other things published by Chapman and Vanguard. Recordings by Tower Records, Argo (among others, a jazz anthem by the Michael Garrett Sextet and Donald Swann—"Morning Service") and Pye.

They have found their way into courses of religious instruction, retreats, school services and young people's Masses. 1963 saw the first performance of a jazz Mass composed by Peter Janssens.[13] There was much activity in 1964 and 1965, as parochial communities began to participate in the spirited new Masses for young people. Some groups of older students also sang negro spirituals, using English lyrics.

Much of the initiative for these new songs in the liturgy came from priests who were working with young people. They usually borrowed the melody of a spiritual or chanson and composed new lyrics, but they also composed new melodies, based on popular tunes or church hymns. Amateur bands usually provided the instrumental accompaniment, leading people to erroneously label these Masses as "jazz" Masses.

Some professional musicians have also contributed to this effort. Peter Janssens, a young composer of theater musicals, has been particularly active in this respect. Two cathedral organists, Ludwig Doerr (Speyer) and Heino Schubert (Essen), have contributed original compositions to liturgical services for young people; however, they have had some reservations about doing this. On the whole, the new compositions show a wide range of quality in technical expertise and authentic sentiments.[14]

[13] Rochus Hagen, *Jazz in der Kirche?*, p. 29.

[14] See footnote 6 and the following: (a) Protestant works: "Überdenk ich die Zeit," *New Religious Songs 1965;* "Herr, wir bitten," *New Religious Songs 1966;* "Neue geistliche Lieder," edited by Oskar G. Blarr, Christine Heuser and Uwe Seidel, 1967; "Der Frieden ist unter uns," *New Religious Songs 1967;* complete collection (1968), Bosse Verlag, Regensburg. "Bausteine für den Gottesdienst," edited by Jochen Schwarz, Musik der Evangelischen Jugend Deutschlands, Series XIX, Vol. 1-4, choral pieces D 5-8; Paul E. Ruppel, "Crucifixion," Lenten meditation, based on the negro spiritual, for narrator, lead singer, choir, trumpet and contrabass (Die Kantate, No. 97); Neue Lieder für Jugend und Gemeinde (Geistliche Chormusik, Series II, 25); all available from Hänssler Verlag, Stuttgart-Hohenheim. Records: eight records with songs from the series "Bausteine für den Gottesdienst", Aussaat Verlag, Wuppertal (BFC 101-108); "Von Zeit zu Zeit"/ "Wenn Gott es will", Chansons by and with Eva Vargas (Cantate 659 401); "Einst war die Welt"/ "Er offenbart sich überall", Rock piece by Claus Stremmel and Eric Hein (Cantate 659 402); Christmas songs by Martin G. Schneider, Uwe Born Choir, Hamburg (Cantate 659 403); New Communal Songs

FRANCE: Paul Zurfluh reports that there have been many experiments attempting to introduce new musical styles into young people's Masses. Songs have been composed by John Littleton, Father Debaisieux, Robert Fau and Jef Gilson. Masses have been composed by Father Akepsimas, Father Debaisieux and Robert Fau. Except for a few texts by Didier Rimaud and Father

by Martin G. Schneider, Uwe Born Choir, Hamburg (Cantate 659 404); "Halleluja, Billy", songs from the musical by Helmut Barbe (Cantate 643 262); "Vater unser"/ "Keiner, der die Harfe schlägt"/ "Lobet den Hernn, alle Völker", Text by Christine Heuser, Music by Oskar G. Blarr (Schwann AMS Studio 15 017); "Diese Stunde, Deine Zeit" (Schwann AMS Studio 15 019); "Gott schenkt Freiheit", songs from young people's services compiled by Dieter Trautwein (Schwann AMS Studio 15 018); "Einige Leute loben den Frieden", songs from young people's services compiled by Dieter Trautwein (Schwann AMS Studio 15 020); "Auferstanden bist du": a young people's service compiled by Martin Ohly (Schwann AMS Studio 15 023); "Lobe den Herrn", I (Life-Record D 1114, Ingo Engelsmann Sound Studio, Castrop-Rauxel); "Lobe den Herrn", II (Life Record E 603, Ingo Engelsmann Sound Studio, Castrop-Rauxel). (b) Catholic works: Missa cantata, "Herr, rühre meine Lippen an". Lyrics by Christine Heuser, music by Peter Janssens; "Überall wirkt Gottes Geist", Mass songs for Pentecost. Lyrics by Lutz Hoffmann, Franz Mausberg, Karl Norres and Leo Schuhen; music by Peter Janssens; "Alles was atmet lobe den Herrn", 5 psalms for the Mass. Translation by Romano Guardini, music by Peter Janssens; Erste Duisburger Messe, für lead singer, choir, community, combo and organ. Music by Peter Janssens; "Und erbarmt sich seiner Elenden". Four rock hymns for Christmas. Text by Christine Heuser, music by Peter Janssens; "Hymnos akathistos", after an ancient Byzantine hymn to Mary. Music by Peter Janssens (all available from Musikverlag Schwann, Düsseldorf); Ludwig Doerr, New Psalm melodies for lead singer, choir, community, percussion, bass and organ: Ps. 79, 144, 109, 136, Alleluja (Orbis Verlag, Münster in Westfalen); "Unterwegs". New songs of faith for the community to sing. Compiled by the Youth Division of the German Catholic Woman's League (DKF), Bendorf/Rhein. Records: Père Cocagnac, "Deine Augen verraten es mir". Religious and biblical chansons (in German), Schwann AMS Studio 501; "Père Cocagnac singt" (in German), 6 records, Schwann AMS Studio 15001-15006; "Immerfort will ich singen". New songs of faith from Duisburg: "Freut euch, der Herr ist nah"/ "Komm, Herr"/ "Kommt, sagt es allen Leuten"/ "Lass uns nicht allein"/ "Er lässt uns niemals verloren gehen"/ "Immerfort will ich singen"/ "Gib uns allen deinen Geist"/ "Propriumsgesänge zum Pfingstenst"/ "Erste Duisburger Messe" by Peter Janssens (Schwann AMS Studio 502); "Herr, rühre meine Lippen an", missa cantata by Peter Janssens, Text by Christine Heuser (Schwann AMS Studio 15007); "Alles was atmet, lobe den Herrn". Five Psalms for the Mass by Peter Janssens. Translation by Romano Guardini

Rozier, the texts have been rather poor; most of them do not stick close enough to the liturgy texts. There is no longer any talk about composing religious chansons.[15]

YUGOSLAVIA: Marijan Smolik informs us that experiments with new religious songs in Slovenian began about ten years ago. They received new impetus from the chansons of Father Aimé Duval. Up to now, most of the new songs are translations of

---

(Schwann AMS Studio 15008); ". . . und erbarmt sich seiner Elenden": Four rock Christmas hymns by Peter Janssens, text by Christine Heuser (Schwann AMS Studio 15012); "Stimmt in das Lob mit ein": Psalms and Meditations for combo, schola and community by Bernhard Krol (Schwann AMS Studio 15 016); "Freut euch, der Herr is nah": missa cantata for Advent (AMS Studio 15 009); "Herr, wir rufen all zu dir": missa cantata for Lent (Schwann AMS Studio 15 010); "Der Herr ist bei uns, Halleluja": missa cantata for Easter (Schwann AMS Studio 15 014); "Überall wirkt Gottes Geist": Mass songs for Pentecost, composed by Peter Janssens (Schwann AMS Studio 15 015); "Erste Duisburger Messe" for combo, schola and community (in German) by Peter Janssens (Schwann AMS Studio 15 013); "Deutsches Proprium zum Kirchweihfest" for choir, schola, organ and other instruments, by Hans Peter Haller (Schwann AMS Studio 15 011); Ludwig Doerr, "Neue Psalmengesänge, I and II (Fono, Münster in Westfalen, HM 17 066 and HM 17 067).

[15] Published by Le Cerf, Le Levain, Fleurus 31, etc. Records: Père Debaisieux and John Littleton, "Rhythmes et joie", John Littleton and the Little Singers of Saint Laurent. Directed by P. Zurfluh. Orchestra and organ—F. Rauber (Studio SM 17 M-259); John Littleton, "Donnemoi la main, mon frere": John Littleton, the G. Malé trio and the Little Singers of Saint Laurent. Directed by P. Zurfluh (Studio SM 17 M-253); Raymond Fau, "Cantiques pour aujourd'hui": with a chorus of young people. Arrangements by G. de Courreges (Studio SM 17 M-282); Père Akepsimas, "Alleluja, eternel est son amour". Choral parts by the Fontaines/Chantilly Students and the Jef Gilson Group. Soloist W. Chancy (Studio SM 17 A-295); Les Preachers, "Seigneur, voici l'heure". Rhythm ensemble and organ (Studio SM 17 M-294); Raymond Fau, "Mass for Young People." The Little Singers of Nancy under the direction of Cl. Jacquot. With guitar accompaniment (Studio SM 17 M-267); M. Debaisieux, "Joie de ma jeunesse", a Mass. With John Littleton and a choir of young people, a rhythm section and organ. Under the direction of Francis Le Maguer (Studio SM 30-286). On the flip side, the orchestra plays an instrumental version without voice accompaniment; J. Akepsimas, "Battez des mains", a Mass. With Wilbert Chancy. Choral parts by the Fontaines/Chantilly Students and the Jef Gilson Group, under the direction of J. Akepsimas (Studio SM 17A-276). Other records are put out by Unidisc and other record companies.

German or French works rather than original creations, and they are usually based on a recorded version of the song. Both the translations and the original creations are the work of priests for the most part, and professional musicians have not taken part.

The pastor in Stranje has a musical ensemble composed of organ, trumpet, contrabass, three electric guitars, percussion instruments, a children's choir and a mixed choir. He maintains that the rhythms of his music derive from native folk music, not from jazz or rock and roll.

The only published anthology of songs is that of Franc Cerar, S.J. (*Zapojmo, bratje*), which has had a wide circulation. It contains translations of French songs (Duval, Soeur Sourire), German songs (Albert Fleury) and English spirituals; it also contains the Kyrie and Offertory of a jazz Mass by Father Jože Tovšak, and songs by him and Father Franc Cerar. In granting his Imprimatur, the bishop of Maribor required that the editor's Foreword expressly prohibit use of these songs in the liturgy. Gradually, however, young people have begun to sing these songs at Mass. The ecclesiastical authorities have winked at the practice.

In Croatia, a vocal and instrumental group (*Zeteoci*) from the theological seminary in Zagreb has won great popularity among young people. However, they do not sing at liturgical services. In 1968, the parish of St. Blaze in Zagreb began to use jazz elements in the music of the Mass. The Catholic newspaper in Croatia, which comes out twice a month, makes no mention of such experiments. It does not provide any information on books, records or conventions that deal with these problems.

ITALY: In April 1965, a concert performance of a "Young People's Mass" took place in the Sala Borromini (Rome). It started a lively debate in the Rome press. During a convention of the *Amici di Catechesi* in Turin (September 1966), one evening was devoted to *canzone spirituale;* a liturgical service on the Word of God was also held, and it included new religious songs.

According to the report in the periodical, *Il Canto dell'Assemblea*, many participants felt that religious concerts were the proper place for such experiments, and that new liturgical music would have to derive from such new songs. Many also wondered why some of the new songs should not be used in the liturgy. They felt that the distinction between sacred and profane was often an illusory one, cherished by people who were reluctant to abandon a dead liturgy for life in the real world.[16]

On December 28, 1967, a *Missa Alleluja* was celebrated during a student convention in Assisi. With music by Marcello Giombini and text by Gino Stefani, it was arranged for voice parts, organ, electric guitars and percussion instruments. In April 1968, three performances of this Mass were given as part of the seasonal program of Milan's Piccola Scala. The program also included Palestrina's Mass, *Lauda Sion,* and Eddie Hawkin's *Missa Nobis* (sung by the "Folkstudio Singers"). In March 1968, the cardinal vicar of Rome granted permission for the use of such songs and instruments at Sunday Mass in the Church of St. Alessio.[17]

SPAIN: Alberto Taulé reports that the new songs are mostly translations or adaptations of negro spirituals. They are also translating German songs that were written for the Tutzing Academy contests, and French songs composed by Father Debaisieux and Father Guy de Fatto. In Catalonia, American folk singers (Joan Baez, Pete Seeger, Bob Dylan, Peter, Paul and Mary) are very popular. Some of these songs have been trans-

[16] *Il Canto dell'Assemblea* (1966), 8:35.
[17] Publications: Adriana Mascagni, "Grazie, Signore"/ "Al Mattino"/ "M'ha esaudito il Signore"/ "Questo giorno"; and Gino Stefani, "Guarda, Signore"/ "È risorto: Alleluja"/ "Tornerà Gesù"/ "Se tu sei libero" (Torino-Leumann). Records: Adriana Mascagni, "Grazie, Signore"/ "Al Mattino"/ "M'ha esaudito il Signore"/ "Questo giorno (LDC 45/14); Gino Stefani, "Guarda, Signore"/ "È risorto: Alleluja" (LDC 45/12); Gino Stefani, "Tonerà Gesù"/ "Se tu sei libero" (LDC 45/13); "Messa Alleluja". Music by Marcello Giombini, Text by Gino Stefani. (Pro Civitate Christiana, Assisi, PCC MS 057-45 EP and 058-45 EP); "Messa Alleluja", Christmastide, Music for the Introit and during the readings (PCC MS 059-45).

lated and adapted for actual use in the liturgy. More recently, Spanish composers have been writing songs in this genre. Among these composers are Manuel Manzano, Kiko Arguello, and Alberto Taulé.

Jazz is not used very much. During the 1967-1968 school year, several experiments were tried in the Jesuit theology school at St. Cugat del Vallés (Barcelona). The general conclusion was that real jazz is not in line with the national character. It did not make it easier for the people to participate, and only a small minority seemed to appreciate it.

Experiments with new songs in the liturgy began during the 1966-1967 school year, and picked up steam the following year. Youth groups and students provided the stimulus, and the experiments took root in rural parishes where guitars were more readily available than organs. Among the promoters of such experiments are Miguel Manzano in Zamora, the Brothers of Christian Doctrine in Salamanca, and the seminary in Seville.

So far, most of the experiments have been tried in the diocese of Barcelona. They were initiated by a lay group (CICF) and by Jesuit theology students, being held in the chapel of the Marian Congregation in Barcelona. Now several parishes use the new songs in their Sunday Masses. It is evident that adults as well as teenagers have found satisfaction in the new services.

There are several different prototypes for the new music: the negro spiritual, American folk songs, pop music and jazz. Most of the new experiments, it seems, are based on folk songs, which are best suited to the local population. Jazz, which requires a good soloist or a good choir, is taking a back seat.[18]

[18] Publications: In the official anthology of liturgical music in Catalan, songs of this type were also included. Among them were translations of "Nobody Knows" (Ficha 13); "Danke" by Martin G. Schneider (Ficha 101); Psalm 148 by P. Debaisieux (Ficha 293); and Psalm 116 by Alberto Taulé (Ficha 282). Records: (a) in Spanish. Manuel Castillo, "Misa Andaluza" (Pax 3064); Kiko Arguello, "Cantos al Misterio Pascual" (Pax C 3094); Miguel Manzano, "Salmos para el pueblo" (Pax Y 701 and L 322); Tino Contreras, "Misa en jazz" (Pax J 409); Spirituals "Tras el rastro de Dios" (Pax J 3116); (b) in Catalan: "Espirituals negres"; "Lloeu el Senyor"; Alberto Taulé, Canticos del nostre temps (Concéntric TC 6090).

PUERTO RICO: In 1965 there appeared a recording of a Mass by Pedro Escabí, which utilized motifs of Puerto Rican folk music and guitar accompaniment. The Mass was sung by the Sisters of the Instituto Religioso de Jesús Mediador, a new congregation dedicated to promoting liturgical renewal and the Church's social doctrine.[19]

BRAZIL: José Weber points out that the pre-existing situation in Brazil differed markedly from that in Europe and the United States. The role of jazz is minimal. Something similar to jazz in origin and makeup exists in Brazil, but it has its own peculiar traits. Brazilian folklore maintained living contact with modern civilization, adapting itself to a technological society. Indeed the new technology helped to shape a common folk music shared by all Brazilians. The songs of the northwest are familiar to people in southern Brazil, and vice versa.

The music of the negro, who was imported as a slave from Africa up to 1850, has exerted the greatest influence on Brazilian folk music. Many forms of music and dance in Brazil can be traced back to negro music. Other sources of Brazilian folk music are the music of the native Indians and the music of European and Asian immigrants.

Beat music and rock and roll, which came to Brazil as by-products of jazz, found a large response among young people. But these genres, too, have been accommodated to native folk music. The rhythm remains, but the melodics is quasi-Brazilian. As in Europe, the new music has its stars in Brazil. In 1968, the International Song Festival (San Remo, Italy) was won by a Brazilian, Roberto Carlos, who is the idol of the rock generation in Brazil.

In some cities there are young people's Masses involving guitar accompaniment. But the music style is folk rather than jazz or rock. There are songs patterned after the chansons of

[19] Misa en La Menor, composed by Pedro Escabí. Instituto religioso de Jesus Mediador.

Father Duval, but they have a distinctively Brazilian cast. Typical are the songs of Father Jocy Rodrigues and Father José Alves.

The task confronting church musicians in Brazil is to adapt Brazilian folk songs and other indigenous music to the liturgy. This effort is being made by the National Commission for Liturgy and Music. Between 1965 and 1968 four national conventions were held to study various aspects of the problem. It is hoped that such meetings will gradually lead to the creation of liturgical music that is authentically Brazilian, allowing the people to give common voice to their liturgical prayer.

Practical experiments have not yet achieved the desired result, but they are moving forward at a satisfactory pace. One noteworthy compilation, *Povo de Deus,* has already appeared. It contains the Proper of the Mass for all Sundays and feast days of the church year. Each Proper is printed separately, with its own melodies and a brief liturgical introduction based on the *Missel de l'Assemblée Dominicale* (St. Andrew's Abbey, Bruges).[20] There is an accompanying set of records also, but the compilation has not yet been distributed widely.

In the area of catechetics, Father Jocy Rodrigues has compiled an anthology entitled *Evangelho em ritmos brasileiros.* It presents song versions of biblical texts, based on the rhythms of Brazilian folk music.[21]

Summary

These experiments are not isolated local phenomena. They are to be found throughout the Western world and beyond it. The music styles of these experiments are closely related to current fashions in music, but that does not permit one to conclude that the whole phenomenon is simply a fashion craze.

[20] Editôra Vozes, Ltd., Petropolis, RJ.

[21] Jocy Rodrigues, O Evangelho em Ritmo Brasileiro. I: Parábolas. II: Cenas do Evangelho. Edição da Universa laus, Secção Brasileira; a catechetical anthology has been brought out by the Mission Sisters of the Crucified Jesus.

The starting point for these experiments varies greatly from country to country. Two basic objectives seem to lie behind them: (1) to get people singing in their liturgical worship; (2) to introduce modern, popular musical genres into the liturgy. Young people are particularly articulate about this second objective. Both objectives are confronted by a common phenomenon: an international brand of music, varying only slightly from country to country, is being promoted by the media of mass communication.

There is more difference of opinion when it comes to evaluating this music. In many countries, traditional folk music merges quite easily with the popular music of the mass media. Prejudice against this music is naturally stronger in countries where there is a living tradition of church music and classical music. Young people are less prejudiced in this respect than adults.

Social differences no longer play a real role here, for listening habits are no longer conditioned by social class. Indeed, the very young people who are most interested in modern art and avant-garde music find the least discrepancy between mass media music and other forms of music. They see more of a chasm between all the musical forms of today and those of yesteryear.

Many of the new experiments are initiated and supported by high school and college groups. Thus they are championed by educated people, and it is clearly false to pretend that a boorish mob is trying to drag the liturgy down to its level. Nor should we overlook the fact that these are not strictly musical experiments. They are tied up with a broader effort to update and reshape liturgical worship.

Our reports indicate time and again that the young people collaborate with priests in working up these liturgical services. The same point is stressed in reports from the Protestant side: "Most of the young people's services and the experiments with new songs seem to be prompted by a single fact. Many young people no longer seem to regard religious services as formalized fixtures of the institutional Church, which they are to attend as mere spectators. They want to have a hand in shaping and conducting these services. Even when the initiative comes from a youth moderator, pastor or choir master, this fact seems to be taken into account somehow. Many of the services are put together by anywhere from 10 to 80 people. Personal selection of songs is only one element in the process." [22]

The surprising thing is that music and singing are an element in the picture at all. We had no reason to suspect that young people would be so earnest about singing in liturgical services. But the fact is that they have an acute need to sing and to make music when they worship God in the liturgy.

IV

THE ARGUMENTS ON BOTH SIDES

Because of the varying circumstances in different countries, the new experiments are not discussed with equal intensity everywhere. Such discussion is more common in countries that have a tradition of church music behind them. At first much of the discussion took place in the daily press; to compile a bibliography of these discussions would be very difficult and probably fruitless. On the whole, periodicals on church music have been, and still are, reluctant to concern themselves with these experiments.

Up to now the most extensive literature on this topic has appeared in Germany. This seems to be due to the fact that Germany has a long tradition of church music and a well developed line of music publications.[23]

[22] Günter Hegele, *Warum neue religiöse Lieder?* (Regensburg, 1964), 5f.

[23] *Bibliography:* GERMANY (besides the works already cited): Franz Mausberg and Dieter Kaulhausen, *Jazzklänge im Kirchenraum* (Hoppe und Werry, Mülheim/Ruhr); Theo Lehmann, *Negro Spirituals: Geschichte und Theologie* (Eckart Verlag, Witten, 1965); Lothar Zenetti, *Heisse Eisen: Jazz, Spirituals, Beatsongs, Schlager in der Kirche* (J. Pfeiffer, Munich, 1966); *Fantasie für Gott: Gottesdienst in neuer Gestalt* (Kreuz Verlag, Stuttgart); Georg Geppert, *Songs der Beatles: Texte und Interpretationen* (Munich, 1968); Gunter Rutenborn, *Beiträge zur Theologie des Jazz* (Musik und Kirche, 1958, 28:65); Walter Hanft, "Theologie und Schwarze Kunst, *ibid.*, 160; Herman Kobold,

The arguments raised in support of the experiments can be summed up as follows:

1. The liturgy must speak the language of today when it comes to music also. Its music cannot be restricted to one level.

2. The Church has always adopted secular styles, secular music and secular modes of expression, and then transformed them into spiritual forms of expression. Her ability to do this has

---

"Zur Theologie des Jazz," *ibid.*, 169; Hermann Josef Burbach, "Religiöse Schlager: Eine neue Form der Verkündigung oder fromme Schnulze?" (Musica Sacra CVO 85, 1965, 45); Thomas Kohlhase, "Anmerkung zur deutschen SpiritualMesse für die Fastenzeit," *Musica Sacra*, CVO 86, 1966, 178; Volker Hopf, "Schlager in der Kirche?" *Musica Sacra*, CVO 85, 1965, 267; Lothar Zenetti, "Spirituals and Gospel Songs: Eine Möglichkeit für uns?" *Musik und Altar*, 1966, 18:55; Johannes Aengenvoort, "Die Kontrafaktur in der Geschichte des geistlichen Liedes," *ibid.*, 71; Rainer Glen Buschmann, "Neue Klänge in der Kirche," *ibid.*, 84; Richard Kliem, "Bemerkungen zu einzelnen Texten neuer religöser Lieder," *ibid.*, 86; "Jazz in der Kirche," Two letters from the readers (Fritz Schütt and Helmut Hucke), *ibid.*, 182; volume 4 of "Schallplatte und Kirche", a companion volume to "Musik und Kirche," 1968, with contributions from Gerhard Schuhmacher, Martin Hünecke, Jochen Schwarz, Hermann J. Burbach and Dieter Trautwein; a bibliography of Protestant discussions on this subject up to 1964 is provided by Günter Hegele in *Warum neue religiöse Lieder?* (Bosse, Regensburg, 1964). SWITZERLAND. Linus David, "Jazz, Spiritual. Gospel: Übernahme oder Anregung?" *Katholische Kirchenmusik*, 1967, 92:23; Theo Lehmann, "Die Lebendigkeit der Negro Spirituals," *ibid.*, 1968, 93:124. SPAIN: Articles by Alberto Taulé and Miguel Manzano in *Phase*, No. 39, June 1967. ENGLAND: The problems were discussed in two issues of *Church Music*, a publication of the Church Music Association, December 1966 and August 1967. See also *English Church Music: 1963*, published by the Royal School of Church Music; Eric Routley, *Twentieth Century Church Music*. The Royal School of Church Music sponsored a study session "Whither Church Music" in May 1963; the Proceedings are out of print. FRANCE: Articles in the periodical, *Église qui chante*. In March, 1968, a convention was sponsored by the Association Saint Ambroise (Chartres); it dealt with these problems. ITALY: The periodical *Il Canto dell'Assemblea* treated these questions at length in its June 1967 issue, Volume 10. BRAZIL: J. Geraldo de Souza, *Folcmúsica e liturgia*, Editora Vozes, Petrópolis RJ. The publication of various convention proceedings is imminent. This bibliography was worked up from answers to our questionnaire. It makes no claims to completeness.

been one sign of her creative ability and of the power of faith. The music styles that some regard as sacred today are actually older historical forms that have become frozen.

3. Aesthetic standards are not decisive in judging the quality of liturgical singing; nor can we use other standards that are not truly applicable here.

The arguments against the experiments are:

1. Music that has associations with dancing and pop songs is not appropriate for the liturgy.

2. The new music appeals to the senses and the motor system of man. Instead of appealing to his intellectual and spiritual capacities, it deliberately tries to lull them to sleep.

3. Mass media music contains many jazz elements, which spring from a cultural environment that is foreign to Western man.

4. Church music is an art. In Western culture at least, the standard is determined by a tradition of *musica sacra*. We cannot utilize ersatz forms of music that are hardly art forms. Modern man, in the unrest of the present day, must be oriented toward spiritual values and taught to appreciate them.

5. Mass media music is a business product. It is marketed over the airwaves and sold by the star singer. The conditions that give it life preclude its use in the liturgy, even if such use might seem desirable.

Evaluating the Experiments

The quality of the experiments seems to disturb both their opponents and their proponents. This is particularly true where a long tradition provides some point of comparison. The general situation in many places seems to be this: the experiments are regarded with favor and sympathy, but the results to date are far from convincing.

We cannot, on the basis of our questionnaire, provide an over-all evaluation of the quality of the experiments in different countries.

V
Positions Taken by Territorial Bishops

The opinion of various bishops and various episcopal conferences seems to be divided. Some bishops give personal encouragement to the new experiments or are at least sympathetic toward them. Other bishops express reservations or reject them outright. Now and then this gives rise to regulatory prohibitions in neighboring dioceses. As far as we can ascertain from our questionnaire, however, most bishops and episcopal conferences have refrained from adopting an official position.

No Experiments with the Mass

When restrictions are imposed, they usually prohibit such experiments in the Mass itself. As far as we know, the conference of German bishops was the first to take a stand on these experiments. In the spring of 1966, it passed this resolution: "So long as the liturgical aptness of jazz-type music is not clearly established, experiments of this sort are not permitted in the celebration of the eucharist. Experiments at other services are subject to the approval of the local ordinary." [24] This resolution was preceded by position papers from various individual bishops. A year earlier, the archbishop of Cologne enacted this decree: "Negro spirituals, pop music and jazz, as they exist today, do not fulfill the requirements for church music. Therefore, they are not suitable for use in the Mass." [25]

Prohibitions on Instruments

Most restrictions seem to pertain to the use of various instruments in liturgical services. This is a continuation of a long tradi-

[24] *Musik und Altar*, 1966, 18:50.
[25] Church bulletin of the Cologne Archdiocese, 105, 1965, No. 233, 415. On June 13, 1965, a service was held in the Cologne Cathedral, featuring the Amateur Big Band of the Steyler missionary priests. Hagen, *Jazz in der Kirche*, p. 29.

tion of similar prohibitions, which called attention to the kind of music associated with a given instrument and its secular connotations. Certain ideals and standards were also developed for church music. Instruments that did not measure up to these standards, or that were associated with music of a different sort, were banned from use in church.[26]

Alberto Taulé (Spain) reports that the new musical experiments have often been discussed by the Comisión Nacional de Música Sagrada. The prevailing view, however, is not to introduce any new instruments into the liturgy, and the national episcopal conference has not provided any further clarification.

[26] Clement of Alexandria: "We will leave Pan's pipe to the shepherd, and the flute to pagan worshipers of idols." St. Jerome once said that a Christian girl shouldn't even know what a lyre is. A diocesan synod in Milan (1565) permitted only the organ to be played for church music, prohibiting "trumpets, horns and other musical instruments" (Fiorenzo Romita, *Ius Musicae liturgicae,* Turin, 1936, p. 66). In 1725, an Avignon synod forbade the use of warlike instruments, such as kettle drums, but it excluded the trumpet from this prohibition because its tone was well suited to reminding people of the Last Judgment (*ibid.,* p. 88). Benedict XIV's encyclical *Annus qui* (1749) forbade the use of kettle drums, hunting horns, trombones, flutes, piccolos, cymbals, mandolins, and other similar instruments that play theater music (*ibid.,* p. 266). Pius X's Motu Proprio *Tra le sollecitudini* excluded the piano, all raucous instruments, and instruments of light music—such as drums, cymbals, etc.—from church music. In his encyclical *Musicae Sacrae disciplina* (1955), Pius XII approved the use of instruments that were not intrinsically profane, raucous or screechy; he mentioned in particular the stringed instruments as being suitable for the liturgy. The 1958 Instruction of the Congregation of Rites adopted this recommendation on stringed instruments. It also made a distinction between instruments that are closely related to sacred music, hence easily adaptable, and instruments that are generally regarded as associated with profane music. The latter were excluded from liturgical use, as were "automatic instruments", radio, and tape recorders. The *Constitution on the Sacred Liturgy* leaves it up to the local ordinary to decide this question (n. 120). The Instruction *Musicam Sacram* again relates the norms of the conciliar Constitution to the 1958 Instruction, excluding instruments that are generally associated with profane music (n. 63). In the field of music there is no longer any sociological or stylistic distinction between the various instruments. All, including electronic instruments, are available to the musician and composer. Ecclesiastical prohibitions on various instruments present a stumbling block to the artistic development of church music; they do not jibe with the assertion that church music is truly an art.

In Brazil, the use of guitars, accordions and drums in the liturgy is permitted *ad experimentum*. In the Melbourne archdiocese (Australia), use of the "classical" guitar is permitted in young people's services; however, electric guitars, bongo drums and tom-toms are prohibited.

Lists of Permitted Instruments and Songs

A third form of regulating the liturgy is to provide lists of permitted songs and instruments, thereby prohibiting excluded songs and instruments. The archdiocese of Melbourne has adopted this approach also. Besides providing a list of song books that may be used in liturgical services, it has also published a list of additional songs that may be used in the Mass or in paraliturgical services. All new songs must be submitted for approval.

Besides publishing these lists, the archdiocese of Melbourne has set forth the basic principles from which its regulations derive. It notes that music, of itself, is neither sacred nor profane. But in music, as in other art forms, certain styles are felt to be either sacred or profane. The web of associations surrounding a given style of music determines whether it is suitable for use in the liturgy. Music that immediately evokes the dance floor or the theater stage cannot get across a religious theme.

Now this does not rule out the sound of popular music entirely. If such music does not have immediate associations with secular entertainment, if it conveys the dignity and solemnity of a religious lyric, then it can be used in a religious song. Many folk songs, for example, deal with themes and sentiments that can be applied to our supernatural relationship with God. The use of a well-known secular melody is not favored, however, because there are too many secular associations attached to it.

One must also take into consideration the varied types of church services and the varying degrees of solemnity involved. If a brand of music is suitable in a paraliturgical service, that does not necessarily mean that it would be suitable for the Mass. In the Mass we join with the priest in offering Christ and ourselves to the Father. We thus proclaim the mystery of Christ and the Church in the most solemn way possible. The Mass is the most intensive expression of our life, and the music of the Mass must convey this intimate solemnity.

The Melbourne regulations go on to discuss the communal character of the Mass. Because it is the cult of a whole community, the music should appeal to all and not just to one particular group. It should not annoy some of the participants. Various age groups are addicted to various types of music, but the common good must be upheld in the liturgy. There is no good reason why young people should not have their own music in their services, so long as it is liturgically suitable. But they should also be taught to appreciate other forms of church music so that they can participate with adults in the parochial liturgy as well.[27]

Positive Encouragement

In Brazil, experiments with folk music in the liturgy have been directly sponsored by the episcopal conference's commission for liturgy and church music. Just recently in France, the *Centre national de pastorale liturgique* (CNPL) published a statement that approved of young people's Masses. The statement talked about young people's active participation in the Mass, noting that the cast of the Mass service itself should enable them to tie it in with their own experience. It also pointed out that the service should use rhythms and instruments that appeal to young people.

The problem of music and musical rhythms goes even deeper. Young people want the Mass to be a unified and dynamic activity. Thus it is most important that preparations for Mass be made with great care, and close attention must be paid to every detail. There must be close and active collaboration between priest and laity, and the experience of youth moderators can contribute a great deal in this area.

Young people are not looking for their own secret services.

[27] The church music regulations of the Melbourne archdiocese are published in the anthology *Hymns for the Liturgy and Paraliturgies*, with an explanation of recent diocesan legislation concerning liturgical music. Issued by the Melbourne Liturgical Commission.

They are thoroughly delighted when adults participate in their services. All the studies of religious educators indicate that the living, communal expression of our faith is an essential element of it, and the liturgy must fulfill this important function by speaking to young people in modern rhythms. The report notes that such experiments should not stop with the Mass but should be extended to other types of liturgical and sacramental services. Bishops are asked to gather information on what goes on in their dioceses, and to utilize the wise collaboration of competent persons and institutions. The CNPL itself has joined with educators and religious instructors to make a thoroughgoing study of "young people and the liturgy".[28]

VI

OPINIONS OF OUR CORRESPONDENTS

At the end of our questionnaire, the correspondents were asked to give their opinion of the various experiments. These opinions varied, of course, because of differing presuppositions and because of the differences in experiments from country to country. It would be nice to be able to plot these evaluations on a neat scale, but terminological differences and complicated factors prevent this. Some experiments are initiated by an ecclesiastical organism or a liturgical commission; others are worked up by young people and their priests, with or without the help of professional musicians. Moreover, the experiments relate to different music genres; some are based on folk music, some on jazz, some on rock or beat music. All these things make a difference and complicate the process of evaluation.

Approval and Disapproval

Only one correspondent expressed basic opposition to these experiments. Saburo Takata is of the opinion that liturgical music in Japan should take its inspiration from Japanese music and from Gregorian chant instead. Alberto Taulé of Spain has

[28] *La Croix* (July, 11, 1968).

this to say: "If liturgical music is to be the music of the people, then we must pursue this idea to its logical conclusion. There are two basic categories of music today: 'cultivated music' and popular music. Now cultivated music is understood and appreciated by only a small minority; it can be used in the liturgy to create a certain atmosphere, but it cannot be used to get the people to sing in church. The other music available is the music of the mass media, which includes popular music with a certain sound and rhythm. My feeling is that the best way to get the people singing in the liturgy is to inject the new rhythms into liturgical chant. We should exclude, of course, dance tunes, top tunes, movie themes and musical hits—anything which has immediate associations with the secular world. But the style and rhythm of the folk song, for example, seems particularly suited for liturgical adaptation. The texts, too, must be appropriate for the liturgy; they must do more than express some Christian idea."

Anthony Newman (Australia) feels that jazz and beat music is the realm of professional musicians, and that it will not suit most people who participate in liturgical services. Such music may win a larger following, but a lot will depend on the kind of music that Christian musicians compose. Some young people have suggested to him that we should sing the best of the protest songs because the repertory of church music lacks such songs. Folk music is picked up quickly, and most churchgoers seem to like it. It seems to possess a human quality that is lacking in our church hymns. It may well be the organ that is strange to the musical sensibilities of the people at large.

José Weber (Brazil) writes: "The music of the people is the most important tool for making the parochial liturgy a living reality." Such music turns the liturgy and Christianity into a real, living experience. Popular music from other countries should not be excluded from the liturgy either.

Sympathy and Skepticism

Johannes Aengenvoort (Germany) is in favor of the new movements, but he feels that most of the experiments so far have not proved very successful. Paul Zurfluh (France) wonders whether the enthusiasm might not be rather short-lived, but he is in favor of the experiments.

Peter Morison (England) points to the difficult task confronting the clergy, who are ultimately responsible for the liturgy. They must try to make sure that the liturgy is relevant, staying within the permitted range of possibilities. No musical style should be condemned without weighing all factors first. Most traditional church music is meaningless to people today, because it is rooted in a past age and a bygone cultural milieu. If the liturgy is to be immediately relevant to them, if it is to arouse participation on their part, then the words and music must be of their time and place. It may well be that the music of the people is the right direction to take, and attempts must be made to find out when and where that is the case.

On the other hand, simple aping of popular music styles involves some risk. The imitators are usually amateurs to a greater or lesser extent; their attempts to make the liturgy relevant may produce results that are short-lived and ultimately disastrous. Prudence is also necessary, and we must remember what the real objective of these experiments is. The best features of bop, beat and jazz will be integrated into the liturgy somehow. But let no one cherish the illusion that it will be an easy job, or that the halls of heaven will echo the latest fashion in pop music.

Marijan Smolik (Yugoslavia) is not intimately associated with the experiments that have taken place in his country, so he cites the opinions of other authorities. One says: "We must talk to young people in their language. We cannot sing these new songs every Sunday, to be sure, but they should be used sometimes during the year." Another points out that "young people do not want to sing the traditional songs. They want to sing their own new songs. Perhaps we will run the danger of making our cultic worship less rational and more barbaric. The dividing line is not clear-cut, and we cannot be sure where all these experiments will lead."

The Help of Professionals Is Needed

Earlier we mentioned the Italian periodical, *Il Canto Dell'* *Assemblea*. Here I should like to cite a passage from the same article:

> Much water has gone under the bridge since the first experiments were held in the Sala Borromini. . . . We are no longer dealing with abstract hypotheses, but with concrete applications that are noted and encouraged by Church authorities both here and elsewhere. Has the hour of young people struck in the Church? We hope it has, but it will depend on us, and on the wisdom of Church authorities, musicians, and pastors of souls. . . .
>
> Wisdom calls for the courage to open up to the needs and demands of young people, to reject the path of blind conformity and fear. If we are unwilling to take risks or to launch bold initiatives, then we shall be like the unprofitable servant who buried his talent in the ground.
>
> Above all, wisdom calls for love. We must take a vital interest in young people. It is not a question of some musical genre or some particular musical instrument. It is a question of opening the doors of the church to young people and allowing the liturgy to bear fruit.[29]

Stephen Somerville (Canada) feels that the introduction of folk music into the liturgy is a welcome, sound and promising initiative. But he would be disappointed if this initiative continued to grow up alongside traditional liturgical music without being integrated into it. His choristers at St. Michael's Cathedral Choir School (Toronto) do not concentrate exclusively on folk music. They want to express themselves in a vital way in the liturgy and to try new forms, but they like both the guitar and the pipe organ. They sing choral renditions of negro spirituals on occasion, and often use guitar accompaniment for the Gradual

[29] *Il Canto dell'Assemblea* (1968), 13:28.

parts. He hopes that folk musicians and serious musicians will be able to learn from each other, so that they can build bridges between old and young, educated and uneducated, past and future.

The former president of the Church Music Association of America, Rembert Weakland, told the Consociatio Internationalis Musicae Sacrae (Milwaukee and Chicago, 1966) that the new experiments were important and necessary for the development of the liturgy. He stressed the need for professional help in these experiments, and he opposed the notion that the Congress should lay down norms for the universal Church. The proceedings of the Congress showed that this was not yet possible.[30] Said Weakland: "If such stringent norms, as those proposed here, had been laid down in the Middle Ages, then there would never have been an organ or part-singing in the Church. Instead of laying down prohibitions, musicians should make serious contact with theologians and liturgists. They should try to comprehend the meaning of liturgical prayer, the importance of active participation, the relativity of liturgical regulations, and the types of music that are now being used in the liturgy. . . ." [31]

Perspectives

It is not easy for the older generation, and for church musicians in particular, to judge the new experiments fairly. There is the danger that our judgments will not deal with the experiments themselves, but with mass media music in general or jazz as we remember it 30 or 40 years ago. We must remember that many developments have taken place since then and that these music forms have spread far and wide and undergone change and development.

The notion that we can bring about liturgical renewal by sticking to the old and revered forms of church music is clearly false. It is not just that they have grown hoary with age. The fact is that

[30] *The Catholic Messenger* (September 8, 1966).
[31] *America* (September 24, 1966).

our musical environment has changed completely. Music is made differently and it is marketed differently; moreover, a whole new set of listening habits has taken root. A cultural critic may look with suspicion on the new forms of musical culture. He may even reject the music of the mass media and even modern forms of classical music. But the liturgical renewal will have to come to grips with the new forms of music; we cannot pretend that we live in an unchanged world, where the traditional forms continue to exert influence and where mass communications do not exist.

It may sometimes seem that only young people are anxious to see jazz and folk music in the liturgy. And one might point out that this music changes from day to day, like the latest fashions. But the underlying presuppositions that give rise to this music do not change from one day to the next. They remain constant, no matter how quickly the songs may come and go. Besides, who can say what the music of the adult world is exactly?

The surprising aspect of these experiments is not that they are oriented around secular forms of music, but that music and singing are regarded as an essential part of the liturgy. One might have expected that the decline of traditional folk singing and the older music traditions would have ended singing in the liturgy. Instead, the growth of the mass media has given rise to new forms of folk singing and musical expression. People now feel a real need to use these forms in the liturgy, even in places where they never sang in church before. Educated young people in particular have stressed this need.

The task of confronting the new musical environment will not be carried out by simply spicing the traditional forms of church music with jazz or folk music. Here we are at the root of the whole problem, and it has not been solved by the experiments undertaken up to now. When we add a new sound to a psalm, or a new rhythm to an Introit, are we providing a better way for the community to approach God, or are we simply tacking a popular trimming onto an old historical dress? Does a new song in the

Mass more clearly symbolize the spiritual meaning imbedded in our action, or is it merely the expropriation of a popular folk song?

One or two experimental pieces seem to point us in the right direction. The Italian *Messa Alleluja* is one example. It will sound strange to the ears of many, to be sure, yet it is amazing how all the varied songs and music strains in it combine to convey a single unified impression. In like manner, the *Werkgroep voor Volkstaalliturgie* (Amsterdam, Holland) has performed an Easter Vigil liturgy that is quite striking.[32] A reading from the book of Exodus on Israel's plight in Egypt is interrupted by a protest song, where the participating community takes the place of the suffering Israelites. This Easter Vigil service utilizes the most varied music styles, including Gregorian chant, and unifies them nicely.

In short, we cannot use jazz, folk music and other types of modern music to whitewash the faded walls of traditional church music. We must regard them as forms of musical expression that have to be taken seriously in any attempt at liturgical renewal. That, I think, is what the new experiments have to tell us.

[32] Available on Didascalia 12 (Gooi & Sticht, Hilversum, Netherlands).

PART III
DOCUMENTATION
CONCILIUM

Office of the Executive Secretary
Nijmegen, Netherlands

Concilium General Secretariat/*Nijmegen, Netherlands*

Toward a Renewal of Religious Language

I

LANGUAGE AS THE EXPRESSION OF MAN

In spite of the "deniers of meaning", like Lévi-Strauss and Lacan, and the inventor of "outside thought",[1] Michel Foucault, man as such has been readmitted to the language debate, mainly as a result of the studies by Gustave Guillaume[2] and his disciples. Chomsky sees in language the expression of man's psycho-mental structure. This structure provides man with "a genetic code which determines his semantic interpretation. . . . It is . . . as if man had at his disposal 'a kind of grammar which gives birth' to its own language".[3] And thus psycho-linguistics, based on the speaker's implicit knowledge of the language he uses, has reappeared in structural linguistics.[4] Language is therefore an essential factor in man's becoming, not only as the

[1] For "outside thought", see M. Foucault, "La pensée du dehors," in *Critique* 229 (June 1966); *Folie et déraison. Histoire de la folie à l'âge classique* (Paris, 1961); *Les mots et les choses* (Paris, 1966).

[2] Cf. A. Jacob, *Temps et langage* (Paris, 1967). For the linking of language with the psycho-mental system, see G. Siewerth, *Wort und Bild* (Düsseldorf, 1958).

[3] N. Chomsky, "De quelques constantes de la théorie linguistique," in *Diogène* 51 (1965), p. 14; *Syntactic Structures* (La Haye Mouton, 1957).

[4] On linguistic structuralism, see J. Piaget, *Le structuralisme* (Paris, 1968), pp. 63-81.

primordial means by which man expresses his consciousness, but also as the animating and organizing factor in the fields of religion, ethics, social culture, politics, etc.

II
RELIGIOUS LANGUAGE

Religious language has its place in the pluriform system of language, but because it reflects a level of consciousness which is *sui generis,* it leads to a perspective which opens up an "other" approach in his experience of reality. Since religious statements have no original linguistic forms of their own, there is no essentially religious element in linguistics. In the believer's existence language acquires a religious meaning. When language has become religious by being referred to the speaker's faith,[5] it becomes prayer, or witness, or preaching.

"Its basic and original source is a certain intimate relationship with the divine": [6] this intimacy specifies religious language, but as a result it reaches beyond the speaker and becomes unintelligible for the non-believer. It reveals indeed a kind of paradoxical intersubjectivity—namely, the coexistence of the believer and his God at the level where God manifests himself. It thus refers, in its second stage, to a subject which is not man, although this subject expresses itself in words of which man is the immediate subject.

Although religious language also uses the linguistic forms at the cognitive level which refers to error and truth,[7] it belongs more to the level of performance which is "an integral part of the act (which it describes) and gives it its proper form".[8] It is even more precisely "self-implying", "since God addresses him-

[5] F. Theunis, "Hoe spreekt men 'religieus'?" in *Streven* 10 (1968), pp. 1024-25.
[6] J. D. Robert, *Difficultés de croire aujourd'hui* (Paris, 1968), p. 66.
[7] Cf. W. T. Blackstone, *The Problem of Religious Knowledge* (Englewood Cliffs, 1963), pp. 47-73.
[8] J. Ladrière, "Langage auto-implicatif et langage biblique selon Evans," in *Tijdschrift voor Filosofie* 28 (1966), p. 446.

self to man in an event or act which commits him with regard to man and expresses his inward self".[9] In return, starting from his living faith the believer expresses his response to God and, through this response, speaks and commits himself in a religious manner.

III

SOCIO-CULTURAL CODES AND THE EVOLUTION OF RELIGIOUS LANGUAGE

As we said above, the language system finds its genetic code in the psycho-mental structure. Like any other structure it "has the three features of totality, transformations and self-regulation".[10] But these transformations are strictly dependent on the dia-chronistic element introduced by time in its character of irreversible evolution. That is why "the synchronistic system of language is not static: it rejects or accepts innovations according to needs determined by the contrasts or connections of the system".[11] Because of this, the totality which language offers cannot subsist independently of this interplay of its transformations, even though it constantly controls these transformations by the process of composition which gives it its character of a structuring totality. However, since language expresses ("translates") the psycho-mental system where the individual and collective factors of variability play their part, the actual regulation of its transformations "supposes regulations based, not on strict operations . . . but on the interplay of anticipations and feedbacks, the application of which covers the whole of life".[12]

This helps us to understand why the evolution of language operates through successive displacements, leaving room for a certain confusion which is the negative limit of the "tentative" improvement of the individual and collective psycho-mental

[9] *Ibid.*, p. 449.
[10] Piaget, *op. cit.*, p. 7.
[11] *Ibid.*, p. 11.
[12] *Ibid.*, p. 15.

structure. This structure objectifies itself as it penetrates further
into the fields of worldly and human reality in successive socio-
cultural codes—that is, in general views and concepts which
offer a combined interpretation of socio-cultural elements
brought to the fore by evolution and attracting attention for the
time being. The code becomes coherent at the level of the "current language" which expresses it, not by the play of logic, but by
the "signs of the times", experienced as a new increase of the
totality. On this view, the invention of a new code always depends on a new level of consciousness, experienced and symbo-
lized by new kinds of relationship and reference. The "signs" of
each code depend, however, on the interplay of the anticipations
and feedbacks we have mentioned above. They can be a revival
of old signs determined by a new meaning on top of the old one,
or, if they are really new, express new demands made of the
present by the future, and this may provoke a considerable up-
heaval in the existing general view of the world.[13] Our own age
is characterized by such demands made of the present by the
future, and this lends the code and signs we are creating today a
certain provocative power over against the past and an origi-
nality liable to all the risks implied in differing from the past.

The evolution of religious language has its own special features. At the level of his life of faith and of the language which
expresses it, the believer must not let himself be overwhelmed by
the fascination of a break in continuity or lose his balance by
being dazzled by what is new.[14] Religious language is less concerned with passing from one code to another at the horizontal
level and more with helping the community of believers to sink
its roots in Christ. Any superficial yielding to any worldly code
would create a shrinking and leveling down of faith. No doubt
the world of faith embraces and permeates the world in every
way. But while the objects pursued in the succession of worldly
codes remain basically tied up with the occurrence of a shift in

[13] Cf. what M. de Certeau said on this point in "Le langage figuratif,"
in *Etudes* (April, 1968), p. 588.
[14] Cf. *idem,* "Apologie de la différence," in *Etudes* (Jan. 1968), pp.
81-106.

the world-view, the object of the religious conscience and its language remains identical in spite of its passage through the worldly codes. It is always the "same" Christ who offers himself to the community of believers as the God-Man in order to associate it with the divine life and prepare it for the eschatological dimension. Seen in this light the Christian code is determined by an overall view of reality which is not subject to the vicissitudes of time and demands, not the clinging to static categories, but a total faithfulness to the original essence of the faith.

This faithfulness to the very origin of Christian life implies that religious language recoils from the fashion or that kind of snobbery which determines in an ephemeral and sometimes negative way a particular worldly code, though otherwise good and necessary insofar as it expresses a new form of human consciousness. That is why the path of religious language, which is bound to follow the path of the world's language in order to have any concrete meaning at all, must be linked to the peaks of this worldly path without letting itself be brought low by the downward slopes of this path. The community of believers therefore has the duty to criticize constructively that language of the human community of which it is an integral part. In the light of its faith it must not reject but refuse to incorporate in its religious language those incidental symbols which overlay and mask the genuine signs of the time that are indispensable to translate the eschatological signs into the language of time.

IV

RELIGIOUS LANGUAGE MUST BE SET FREE

Religious language is the instrument by which the life of faith expresses itself. The crisis which besets it today is therefore the crisis of a life of faith which no longer knows how to express itself to the world. Cut off from the world by its quasi-impotence to communicate with the world through an adequate language, the community of believers has reached the point where it begins to doubt its own existence and the concrete relevance of its language.[15] In its present state religious language is in the situation of an incredible loss of contact with the evolution of the world. That it has fallen so far behind the events is due, among other things, to an uncritical loyalty to old and even antiquated codes and to an almost servile submission to the traditional theological language of the Scholastic kind. Because of this submission, religious language works at the cognitive level in favor of a scheme of which the theoretical pattern hardly fits the philosophies of existence as well as the human and positive sciences while the new theology takes these philosophies and sciences more and more seriously, even in its own language.

On this basic point the Christian self-awareness needs a thorough examination and must detach itself from out-of-date socio-cultural and linguistic forms by checking its religious language with the demands of a faith lived at the point of its enduring origin—namely, Christ, the God-Man. Any other norm for such a de-mythologization would only lead to a "profanation" of the religious language. But such a self-examination has meaning only insofar as it can bring about a conversion of religious language to the positive elements in the new human code. This code has a capacity for universalization which is far better equipped to express the original essence of the faith than the socio-cultural codes of the past. As the *Constitution on the Church in the Modern World* has admitted, a new collective consciousness has emerged which aspires toward a "full and free life", a truly human existence which uses "all the immense potential offered by the modern world", and expresses itself "in courageous efforts to create some form of universal community" (n. 9). It is concerned with a "general change" which is leading to "a veritable transformation, both social and cultural, with effects that have their repercussions on man's religious life as well" (n. 4).

[15] For the crisis of religious language, see "Le langage et la foi," in *Lumière et Vie* 88 (1968); M. de Certeau, "La parole du croyant dans le langage de l'homme," in *Esprit* (1967), p. 456; F. Theunis, *op. cit.;* P. Roqueplo, "Une foi normalement difficile," in *Science et foi* (Paris, 1962).

Religiousness consciousness must wake up to this transformation and adapt itself by beginning with the transformation of its language.[16] This implies that in itself it must reinforce the commitment to Christ and to God which it finds in the referential points contained in the commitment to a mankind in search of a universal community, beginning with the socialization and democratization of society. The "mythical" symbols which lend a magic-superstitious character to public prayer and devotion, the unhealthy climate of escapist dreams, must yield to the symbols of a freedom which creates its own forms, its own interhuman dialogue where man represents God and finds his image of God, and uses the legitimate human joys that join body and spirit in spontaneous gestures.

[16] For further information on the subject of the renewal of religious language, cf. P. Barthel, *Interprétation du langage mythique et théologie biblique* (Leyde Brill, 1963); H. Boeracker, "De gelovige en het evangeliewoord," in *Tijds. v. Theologie* 1 (1968), pp. 1-20; R. Bultmann, *History and Eschatology* (Edinburgh, 1957); B. Catao, *Renouveau de l'Eglise et langage de la foi* (IDO-C 67-34, Oct. 12, 1967); E. Borne, C. Bruaire, F. Varillon, "Connaître Dieu," in *Recherches et Débats* (Paris, 1965); H. Denis, *Pour une prospective théologique* (Paris, 1967); F. B. Dilley, *Metaphysics and Religious Language* (New York, 1964); G. Ebeling, *Wort und Glaube* (Tübingen, 1960); D. C. Evans, *The Logic of Self-Involvement. A Philosophical Study of Everyday Language with Special Reference to the Christian Use of Language about God as Creator* (London, 1963); H. Halbfas, *Fundamentalkatechetik. Sprache und Erfahrung im Religionsunterricht* (Düsseldorf, 1968); H. G. Hubbeling, "De betekenis van de analytische filosofie voor de wijsgerige theologie," in *Tijds. v. Theologie* (Dec. 1967), pp. 734-69; J. A. Hutchison, *Language and Faith* (Philadelphia, 1963); J. B. Metz, "Die christliche Sprache in unsere Welt," in *Zur Theologie der Welt* (Mainz, 1968), pp. 116-22; H. Mynarek, *Mensch und Sprache* (Freiburg i. B., 1967); J. P. de Rudder, "Gelovig spreken en theologische taal," in *Tijds. v. Theologie* 3 (1968), pp. 260-78; I. Ramsey, *Religious Language* (London, 1967); G. P. Widmer, "Sens ou non-sens des énoncés théologiques," in *Rev. des sciences philosophiques et théologiques* LI (1967), pp. 644-65.

BIOGRAPHICAL NOTES

EVANGELISTA VILANOVA, O.S.B.: Born in Spain in 1927, he was ordained in 1952. He studied at San'Anselmo in Rome and at the Institut Catholique in Paris, receiving his doctorate in theology in 1957. He is professor of dogmatic theology at the Theological Faculty of Barcelona. His published works include "Vías históricas de la autoreflexión de la Iglesia," in *Comentario eclesial a la Ecclesiam Suam,* and "Cinquanta anys de teologia de la liturgia," in *Il Congrés liturgic de Montserrat* (1965).

MARTIN McNAMARA, M.S.C.: Born in Ireland in 1930, he was ordained in 1954. He studied in Rome at the Gregorian and the Biblical Institute, and in Jerusalem at the Biblical Institute and Biblical College. He holds a licentiate in theology, and is a doctor of biblical science and honorary graduate of the Biblical College of Jerusalem. He is professor of scripture to the Missionaries of the Sacred Heart at Moyne Park, Ireland. His published works include *The New Testament and the Palestinian Targum to the Pentateuch* (Rome, 1966).

HANS MEYER, S.J.: Born in Germany in 1924, he was ordained in 1956. He studied at Innsbruck, Salamanca and Rome, receiving his doctorate in theology in 1959. He is professor of moral theology at the Faculty of Theology of Innsbruck University, where he is also dean. He is also president of the Institute of Moral Theology and Social Doctrine at Innsbruck. His published works include *Luther und die Messe* (Paderborn, 1965) and *Lebendige Liturgie* (Innsbruck, 1966). He is editor in chief of *Zeitschrift für katholische Theologie.*

SALVATORE MARSILI, O.S.B.: Born in Italy in 1910, he was ordained in 1933. He studied at San'Anselmo in Rome, receiving his doctorate in theology in 1938. He is professor of theology and liturgy at the Pontifical Liturgical Institute in Rome, where he is also the director. His published works include *La Messa* (Turin, 1960).

GINO STEFANI: Born in Italy in 1929, he is a Catholic. He studied in Spain at the University of Comillas, and in Italy at both the Institut de Musique Sacrée and the Conservatoire in Milan. He received his doctorate in philosophy, and a degree in composition and polyphony. He is a musicologist who composes music and hymns. His published works

181

include *L'Espressione vocale et musicale nella liturgia* (Turin, 1967). He is also the author of numerous articles on sacred music in pastoral liturgy.

KILIAN MCDONNELL, O.S.B.: Born in the U.S.A. in 1921, he was ordained in 1952. He studied at the Catholic University in Washington and in Canada at the University of Ottawa in Canada, as well as in Europe at Tübingen, Münster, Geneva and Oxford. He received his doctorate in theology in 1965. He is director of the Institute of Cultural and Ecumenical Research at St. John's Abbey, Collegeville, Minn., and is also professor of theology at St. John's University, Collegeville. His publications include *John Calvin, the Church and the Eucharist* (1967).

JOS LESCRAUWAET, M.S.C.: Born in Amsterdam in 1923, he was ordained in 1948. He studied at the Catholic University of Nijmegen, receiving his doctorate in theology in 1957. He is professor of dogmatic theology at the Faculty of Theology in Tilburg. His published works include *De Bijbel over de christelijke eenheid* (1961) and *Compendium van het Oecumenisme* (1962).

COLIN BUCHANAN: Born in London in 1934, he was ordained in the Anglican Church in 1962. He studied at Tyndale Hall Theological College, gaining his M.A. in 1962. He is librarian and lecturer at the London College of Divinity. His publications include *Modern Anglican Liturgies* (Oxford, 1968).

HEINRICH RENNINGS: Born in Germany in 1926, he was ordained in 1955. He studied at the universities of Münster and Innsbruck, and at the Institut Superieur de Liturgie in Paris, receiving doctorates in philosophy and theology. He is dean of studies at the Liturgical Institute at Trier in Germany, and coordinator of pastoral liturgy. His publications include *Richtlinien der deutschen Bischöfe für die Messe* (Münster, 1962), and *Kommentar zur Instruktion "Inter Oecumenici"* (Münster, 1965).

HELMUT HUCKE: Born in Germany in 1927, he is a Catholic. He studied at the Ecole Supérieure de Musique at the University of Freiburg im Breisgau where he received his doctorate in philosophy in 1952. Since 1966 he has been director of Church music at the Liturgical Institute at Trier in Germany. His publications include "Das 'munus ministeriale' der Musik im Christlichen Kult," in *Kirchenmusik nach dem Konzil* (Freiburg, 1967).

International Publishers of CONCILIUM

ENGLISH EDITION
Paulist Press
Glen Rock, N. J., U.S.A.

Burns & Oates Ltd.
25 Ashley Place
London, S.W.1

DUTCH EDITION
Uitgeverij Paul Brand, N. V.
Hilversum, Netherlands

FRENCH EDITION
Maison Mame
Tours/Paris, France

JAPANESE EDITION (PARTIAL)
Nansôsha
Tokyo, Japan

GERMAN EDITION
Verlagsanstalt Benziger & Co., A.G.
Einsiedeln, Switzerland

Matthias Grunewald-Verlag
Mainz, W. Germany

SPANISH EDITION
Ediciones Guadarrama
Madrid, Spain

PORTUGUESE EDITION
Livraria Morais Editora, Ltda.
Lisbon, Portugal

ITALIAN EDITION
Editrice Queriniana
Brescia, Italy